Living
Loving
&
Unlearning

**A therapist's guide to healing and living
authentically from the inside out.**

Cynthia Brennen, LMSW

Living
Loving
&
Unlearning

**A therapist's guide to healing and living
authentically from the inside out.**

Cynthia Brennen, LMSW

Published by Weintraub & Messinger
2014

ISBN 978-1-304-61230-4

Published by Weintraub & Messinger
New York, NY

www.CynthiaBrennen.com

For my father, Norman James Weintraub, who always encouraged me to be the person I was born to be. I feel your healing from the heavens, Dad. Thank you for blessing me with your unconditional love.

Contents

I.
~Living in Authenticity~

II.
~Self-Love~

III.
~Journey to Change~

IV.
~Soul Connectors~

V.
~Our Sacred Gift~

VI.
~Healing the Broken Heart~

VII.
~Letting Love In~

VIII.
~Darkness Leading to Light~

IX.
~Allowing the Unknown~

X.
~Body and Mind~

XI.
~In My Life~

XII.
~Spirit Song~

XIII.

~Earth Angels and Beyond~

XIV.

~Bringing it Home~

"I went to the woods because I wished to live deliberately, to front only the essential facts of life, and see if I could not learn what it had to teach, and not, when I came to die, discover that I had not lived."

~Henry David Thoreau

Foreword

I first became aware of Cynthia and her work in early 2011. My own journey through a severe mental breakdown, depression and an eventual diagnosis of Bipolar Disorder had left me searching for answers and healing. At every opportunity I read books, researched websites, listened to interviews and experienced a number of different holistic treatments to regain my physical, mental and spiritual well-being. This has been a daily and most rewarding journey.

I found Cynthia initially through her website and then on Facebook (Isn't social media a wonderful thing!). Her attitude toward life, recovery, healing, and the infinite possibilities we all have available to us to regain and maintain good health resonated with me immediately. From there, I sent Cynthia a message. I'm based in Australia, and in the past nine years have written two books and shared my story to many audiences around the country. My aim is to educate, reduce stigma around mental health issues and to inspire people to realise the possibilities they have to heal and thrive. Cynthia replied and the rest is history.

I have appeared twice as a guest on Cynthia's radio program in the US and she has been very generous in sharing my story of recovery with her audience and her followers via her website and on social media. In Cynthia's healing book, *Living, Loving and Unlearning*, she will now have the potential to change many more lives for the better. I cannot recommend her work more highly and it will definitely become an important part of my "well-being library."

Craig Hamilton
Author of *Broken Open* and *A Better Life*
Motivational Speaker
Newcastle, Australia

Testimonial

Cynthia Brennen is a very proficient and capable counselor. She even has four letters following her name to prove she has trained for and earned that position. To have worked with Cynthia is to know that she is much more than a counselor. She has the innate ability to bring to others the realization of their true capabilities, to empower them to find purposes and callings for a fuller, richer life. She is a conduit to the path of peace, love, harmony, and inner health. What Cynthia has to say, whether over radio, within written pages, or in everyday conversation is worthy of our attention. In the past she has brought forth a better environment, mentally and physically, for those hurting, weakened, bruised or broken. She continues to do this, and do it well. The opportunity to receive Cynthia's impartations is no less than the reader being handed a candle in the dark.

Carolyn S. Hennecy
Author of *Orange Blossom Wishes; Child Molested, Woman Abused ~ Her Victorious Journey to Freedom*
Designated Victim Services Practitioner
Domestic Violence Victim Support Advocate
Keynote Speaker and Consultant

Acknowledgements

First and foremost, I would like to thank my husband, Michael, and our three beautiful daughters, Kelley, Becca, and Rachel, for their unwavering patience as I spent many hours, days, and years compiling writings for this book. Your understanding is appreciated more than you know.

To my talented daughter, Kelley; thank you for sharing your beautiful artistry in the creation of my book cover. Your feather photo blended with the water, and soothing green flowing into white, couldn't be more perfect. A combination of many messages contained between these pages. Your dad and I were blessed the day you and your sisters flew into our lives.

God only knows when this book would have come to fruition if it weren't for one very special person, Marjie Messinger; my four-year roommate at Ithaca College, my driving force, my efficient organizer, and most of all, my true friend. We were blessed the day the universe joined us together in that corner room of Holmes Hall. Fast-forward thirty years: Marjie and I were sitting in a sweet café overlooking Central Park, sipping our hot cocoa and discussing her business name, "I Can Do That," and all she does for small businesses and organizations. I turned to her and asked, "Can you get my book published?" She immediately responded, "I can do that!" There was no doubt in my mind Marjie could "do that" and more. She created the layout, edited, and lined up my publication with efficiency and flair! Words could never express my gratitude to you, Marjie, for literally putting this book together. I always knew we made a great team, roomie.

Many thanks go out to the thousands of clients I have had over the last 30 years, along with all the guests on my talk radio show, *Help, Hope & Healing.* You have all been an amazing inspiration in my writing and transformation of this book. A big thank you to Backyard Broadcasting in Elmira, New York, for providing me the opportunity to reach the masses with my message of health and healing through my guests, and personal and professional experiences. My hope is that this book will help to heal even more people traveling their journey.

Prologue

I was dying. My heart and soul, that is. I couldn't breathe. I felt lost in a world that whirled around me. If I didn't make some changes soon I knew I would be gone. It was now or never. I had to find the key to unlock my imprisoned spirit, she was crying out to me for help! My first hint was when I landed in my doctor's office with heart palpitations. I rode the treadmill, performed all the cardiac stress tests and did everything they told me to do. In the end, my doctor looked at me and simply said, "It's stress." Yep, as simple as that, stress. I knew in that moment my life had to change. I was killing myself, and for what? Running around like a chicken to make sure everyone was happy; everyone but me, that is. I wanted everybody to like me and see what a hero I was, but "appearing" to be the hero nearly killed me.

I woke up. And then the work began…

I had written the above in my journal 11 years ago, as I reflected on the day my life changed. I had just turned 41. Since then I have searched, created, and lived a life devoted to discovery. In this search there have been many bumps in the road, and just as frequently, beautiful balloon rides. Self-discovery is an amazing experience, requiring dedication to the unveiling of your authentic self. It has been said, the truth will set you free. This much I know is true, realizing YOUR truth will set your soul free. It is through this process that I have created balance in my life, focusing on mind, body, spiritual, and emotional wellness. In living this delicate balance, I have experienced many trials and errors in my life, and I feel blessed and honored to be a guide in my clients lives as they unravel their own discoveries. It is only through my willingness to experience life to the fullest that I am able to support my clients unconditionally as they travel their own roads.

This book is a compilation of my writings over the past four years. I delve into spiritual and emotional wellness, exercise and nutrition, mental health, and personal and professional experiences through all of it. The process of unlearning is a key component of my writing, as it focuses on peeling away the layers put upon us by society and individuals in our life, and rebuilding the real you. The soul you were born to be on this earth. Simply, the purity of yourself.

With Love and Blessings,

Cynthia

Introduction

The pages contained in this book are like a mixed bag of angel cards. You know, the kind of book where you can close your eyes, take a deep breath, and randomly open to a page meant for you on that day, at that moment. It can certainly be read front to back for lessons of learning and unlearning, but if you're looking for a lesson in the moment, give it a try. You just might receive a message that uncannily relates to your life, inspired by the universe, reaching deep into your soul. Happy reading. ~Namaste

I.

Living in Authenticity

"Whatever course you decide upon, there is always someone to tell you you are wrong. There are always difficulties arising which tempt you to believe that your critics are right. To map out a course of action and follow it to the end requires courage."
~Ralph Waldo Emerson

The Process of Unlearning

The process of unlearning. A concept that may sound a bit strange to you at first, especially since so much emphasis has been put on learning throughout our lifetime, but if you consider the expectations put upon us by influential people in our lives, you may begin to understand the meaning behind this reversing process.

When we entered this world as babies, with the purity of our untouched souls encased in our bodies, we were completely free. Free of judgment, expectations, and totally accepting of who and what we were. We flailed with joy, extending our limbs out from our soul to feel and experience the world around us. We cried when our tummies were hungry, we needed a diaper change, or a good burp to let out some air. Pretty simple. Then piles of learning came upon us. We needed to learn a plethora of skills just to survive in this world. In addition, the teachers in our lives taught us beliefs they thought were important; often beliefs they were taught and so on down the line. The question remains; is what our teachers were taught attributes that resonated with our personal soul? Very likely, some did and some did not. Your challenge today is to dig down deep into your soul and tune in to what resonates with your authentic self. As you do this you will strip away the layers of all those expectations you piled on to please others. Anything that doesn't feel comfortable in the pit of your gut is worth reevaluating in your life. I use the metaphor of peeling away the layers like a banana peel, discarding one strip at a time. As you do this you create room for the real you! What would you add to your life as you strip away the old? Listen to the whispers of your soul and you will begin to live the life you came here to live. Fulfilling your purpose here on earth.

The more you become the purity of your soul the happier you will feel walking your earthly journey. Enjoying your own path as you extend your natural love and positive energy out to others. Just as you were meant to be, living in the vastness of simplicity. To be true is to be you.

Enhance Your Balance!

Balance is the golden key in life. If you move too much in either direction it can be detrimental to your health. Keeping the pendulum swinging and remaining centered is what will meet your needs physically and mentally.

Listen when your intuition speaks. It will let you know when you are out of balance. While I was training for my Hero Rush run and swim meets (more on these events later), I was in the best physical condition I had been in a long time, but my knee was beginning to hurt and I pulled my thigh muscle. As much as my competitive mind told me to keep going, my ego-less intuition told me to rest. I ended up listening to those little angels on my shoulder and guess what happened? My thigh muscle healed and my knee pain (which was becoming chronic) healed itself too. This wasn't from taking a day or two off, it was from doing very light workouts throughout the summer. I am now ready to begin swimming with the team again with no concern over physical ailments turning permanent. Rest is good. Listen when your angels speak to you.

The same holds true for our nutritional, spiritual, and emotional health. You know when you've fallen off track. It's up to you to make the decision to get back on the train to wellness, or not. Your body, mind, and soul will always let you know what is lacking. Pay attention and your life's journey will flow with ease. Whenever we feel secure and healthy in our own skin and soul, life rolls. Swing on your personal pendulum and be mindful of your center. Your peaceful place. Your home.

In the Now

I recently heard yet another story about a popular figure who lived an extremely healthy lifestyle and still was hit by cancer and passed on. As I listened to this commentary my thoughts drifted into the silliness of any of us thinking we can cheat death or control the time we exit this earth. Any of you who know me, know that I live as healthy as I possibly can in all areas of my life. Do I do it because I want to live forever? No, I do it because I want to live in the now! Each day, every moment, is something to be treasured. Of course we all have down times; that's part of life and our ever-present learning curve along our journey, but to travel with a clear mind and heart takes your journey to a whole new level. I certainly want to be alert in my growing and remember what I have learned. Some to be experienced again and some to be avoided like the Black Plague.

My point is this; to live healthfully is to live in this moment. Notice that which surrounds you. The beauty, the messages, your loved ones, your insights, and the clarity that comes with all of it. Live healthy simply because it allows you to feel full of energy with happiness in your life. Live it because it gives you a new perspective in seeing the glass full as life shoots you lemons. Live it because it feels good!

When our time comes to move into the spirit world it is a day of celebration for a life well lived and a bow of gratitude for a life yet to come. Feel it, breathe it, BE it now, for this is it. Your time to show yourself and shine!

Stop, Drop, and Roll

In an emergency fire, the experts recommend that you stop, drop, and roll to give you a better chance of survival and save your life. I recommend the same in keeping with the survival of our spiritual wellness. Preventative damage control is crucial to keeping our soul in balance. Out of balance, and we are likely to get burned.

Stop! Stay in the present moment. Right now you don't need to worry about the past or the future. Sit with now and allow the energy of life to flow to you. Look at your feet. That's where you are, all is well and good and that's all you have to think about in this moment. If your concerns start to take over, bring yourself back to the present. Each step you take in this moment will bring you to your intended destination.

Drop to your knees! As painful as it may seem to be, humility is nourishment for the soul. It is when we are humbled that we finally see the forest through the trees. Our hearts open and we see the light in others more. We tend to give more and feel fulfilled in our daily life. It is when the ego takes control that we begin to feel the emptiness. The ego is not always a bad thing, it can spur you on to reach certain goals, but when it is leading your life it depletes your spirit. The ego constantly searches for outer approval and will trample on others to hear the applause. It's a lonely road back to reality.

Roll with the tide...allow life to ebb and flow, and expect that it will. We all have ups and downs. When the "downs" come, know that it won't stay that way forever. It is in the down time that we gain strength and learn to appreciate the "ups" of life! The light is so much sweeter when we've recently experienced the dark. Roll, don't control.

And lastly, but certainly not least, add in a little rock 'n ROLL and enjoy the fun flow of life!

LOVE

"We do not know but we can LOVE. LOVE is easy, fear is hard." ~The Silence

When we fight love, out of fear, life becomes very unsettling. It is sometimes difficult to allow yourself to become vulnerable when you've been hurt many times, but don't allow the hurts to imprison you. It is the openness that fosters growth, even if painful along the way. I am very firm about the importance of boundaries, but if we completely block ourselves due to fear, the sadness turns inward and becomes harmful to the heart. Be open and treat yourself with kindness. Live life with love. The more we have love in our lives, the more we have God in our lives, and THAT is the warmest place to be. God is Love.

For those of you who don't know, The Silence is a wise woman who was in my life for a short time. She crossed through the veil a few years ago and still lives inside of me. She created a collection of beautiful cards that surround me in my office, and on certain days, I close my eyes and pull a card. Always full of love, spirit, and wisdom. A warming in my heart. She guides me to this day.

The Power of Affirmations

What we think, is what we become. Who we spend time with, is the vibrational energy we emit. What we surround ourselves with, is how we feel. Where we spend our time, manifests our life force.

My friend gave me a beautiful blue stone. We call it my "Pisces" stone as it throws off the colors of the ocean. It sits on the dashboard of my car, reminding me of our friendship and the ease of the cool big blue.

I have a thing for hearts and anything embracing light and love. Simple things like the scent of a rose, the touch of a hand, the chirping of a bird, brings a smile to my face. I don't abhor darkness, as it is a piece of life. I deal with it, and I move on.

As I moved through the vinyasas in my yoga class this morning, I imagined letting go of all that I cannot control. Feeling gratitude that life sends me these challenges to learn from. When I released, my heart opened, creating a beautiful inner peace.

Now, as I sit in my favorite cafe, savoring my favorite artichoke soup, I feel joy as I write, soaking it all in. Tonight, I'm meeting up with some wonderful friends I haven't seen in a long time. One thing I know for sure, there will be a lot of laughter in that room!

I'd say that this day is full of affirmations of joy, light, peace, health, and love. Affirm your daily existence and breathe it in. You have the POWER to create the life you live! You are what you think, feel, experience, and believe…

AWE

In our fast-paced culture it is natural to become self-focused. We run so quickly and move to meet the needs of our children, partners, clients, co-workers, pets...the list goes on. By the end of the day we feel depleted. Oftentimes, people will attempt to fill their depletion with outer material things. It's a temporary fix and never fills the inner spirit that requires nurturing.

What does fill the inner spirit is connecting to outer spirit. Step outside of yourself and tune in to the AWE of life! Notice the beauty that nature brings you; don't rush by that butterfly on the vine, stop and notice the color and movement of its wings, recognize the signs that come to you as messages from angels, give gratitude to God when someone thanks you for helping them. Think of, or speak to, loved ones who have crossed through the veil, smell the dew on the trees during your morning run, sloooow down and take it all in. There is NOTHING that fills you or gives you the inner warmth you feel when you truly connect to Spirit.

Keep your eyes, ears, and heart open today, who knows what AWE the universe will bring you!

Enjoying the Passage of Time

If you ever really listen to James Taylor's song, "Secret O' Life," you will feel the mystery, the miracles, the letting go. I picture a free-falling and a trust that Spirit is going to catch me mid-air. It is a trust that you are okay wherever you turn. There are no mistakes, simply lessons and opportunities as we ride the waves. Sometimes, we have to struggle to our feet, scrape ourselves off, and allow healing to take place...then get right back into the tumble. Sometimes, as we flow, miracles happen that we never could have imagined possible. A mystery. Something completely out of our control. So go ahead. Experience LIFE. Go with whatever may come your way. As James reminds us, "Try not to try too hard, it's just a lovely ride."

Only Your Shadow Knows...

The "shadow side" gets a bad rap in our culture. We are expected to think, act, and perform "properly" in our everyday endeavors. People who choose to step out of the box are often frowned upon as strange or touted as troublemakers. I suggest that it is healthy to explore your shadow. In the yin-yang of life how can we have light without dark? How can we experience happiness without sadness? You simply cannot experience the full impact of joy unless you have had immense emotional pain in your life. You appreciate the abundance that much more when you have had nothing.

The late Psychiatrist, Carl Jung, developed theories pertaining to one's shadow. He believed that "in spite of its function as a reservoir for human darkness, or perhaps because of this, the shadow is the seat of creativity." He went on to say that "everyone carries a shadow, and the less it is embodied in the individual's conscious life, the blacker and denser it is."

In other words, get out there and explore your shadow side! Create and allow yourself to be whole. Learn from your lessons as you travel your journey, no one else's, just yours. Some of my most painful experiences in life have been my greatest gifts. Those thoughts that you repress into your unconscious mind will inevitably push to be seen. Don't fight it, embrace it! The fight often causes more turmoil than the release. Learn from it and grow into the wondrous flower you deserve to be. The author Anais Nin has a beautiful quote that reads, "And the day came when the risk to remain tight in a bud was more painful than the risk it took to blossom."

Don't be afraid to blossom. Enjoy life, have fun, allow your own secret thoughts to come to you, devoid of guilt. Be free, express yourself, and don't concern yourself with others opinions of you. It's really none of your business what they think of you anyway. Walk your own spirit path and allow yourself to be guided. You will find your way.

Mirror of Myself

If you are feeling frustrated or angry with someone close to you, I suggest you stop that thought of projection and take a good look at your own reflection. Most often, we subconsciously choose these people to enter our lives in order to learn and work through our own battles. If we are consistently projecting onto others we will never learn what it is we are attempting to teach ourselves. Accept your lessons and learn from them. Just as we practice acceptance and nonjudgment of others, extend the same to yourself. We are meant to learn as we travel this earth. Don't miss the opportunity to look inward and grow with each reflection. Focus on yourself and allow others to experience their own journey. Everyone's road is individual and meant to be their inner schooling.

Step into your travels, feel the joy and pain of all your choices, and allow others to experience theirs. As we become whole individually we will appreciate the works of art that we are, as well as the beauty of others.

Look into YOUR mirror today. What is it that you SEE?

Victim or Survivor?

Which one are you? Are you someone who accepts your position in life and chooses to take responsibility for your actions? Or, are you someone who chooses to blame others for your lot in life? When we choose to be a victim and blame others for messes we have created in our own lives, we remain stagnate in our mire of pain and often spiral downward as we take pity upon ourselves. In blaming others, we erase our innate abilities and abdicate our power to master our own lives. Only you have created what exists in your life, and only you can change it. Until you accept responsibility for your past decisions and current situation, you will remain a prisoner of your negativity. You can lay down, claim defeat, and continue your cycle; or you can stand up, look yourself straight in the eye, and reclaim your life.

The Survivor chooses to create change. The road may be painful and full of patience, but the end result will be one of self-love, self-respect, humility, compassion toward others, and a knowing that you are fulfilling your purpose here on earth. In claiming your life, you become the master of your ship. There is no blame because you know you have the power to create your own life. You're not depending on someone else to steer your ship, you take the wheel and accept full responsibility: the ups, the downs, and the in-betweens. Life can be extremely difficult but when we know we can rely on ourselves to make it through the storm, and have faith that we will, all our perseverance will pay off. As we begin to trust ourselves we attract like-spirited people into our lives. Naturally, our inner circle of support grows and so do we.

Face your fears and seek the inner wisdom that will set you free. Stay on your course, weather your storms, and the sun will shine upon your tattered and treasured ship.

The Purpose in Living

How do you know when you are living "on purpose?" The universe always lets you know. Your life flows effortlessly, all endeavors seem to fall into place and you feel centered and at peace. When you experience this flow, an inner strength ensues and you feel nothing can pull you off your thread. When we are mindful of this, and accept it with grace and gratitude, the flow continues...until the human side of life steps in.

As spiritual beings living a human existence, the reality is that we all fall off our thread at times in our lives. The important thing to remember is that it really is okay. It's called life and experiencing all it has to offer. Some experiences are dark and some are light. Take what you need in this learning and leave the rest. It's never too late to step back on your purpose train and feel the power behind your soul's engine. NO-thing in life is a failure, they are all simply lessons along your path in finding your way. Your truth.

In living your purpose, there will be many bumps in the road. Continue to live and repair the bumps as you move along. With time, and heart, the road will open up for a smoother ride.

Your purpose is now.

Spread Your Wealth

If you were to invest your money, would you put it all in one account or would you diversify? Which do you think would be the wiser choice? In recent economic times, we have seen many individuals and businesses take a nosedive because they put all of their eggs in one basket. Think of your own spiritual and emotional basket. If you put all of your energy into one person what happens when that person dies, or leaves you, or lets you down? Where does that leave you? As I've discussed before, you need to fill your own basket first, but what about your other social networks? Your friends, family, extended family, co-workers, etc. are all a part of you diversifying your spiritual and emotional wealth. What happens to you when someone you are close to shows their "human-ness" and disappoints you? Do you fall apart or do you find your own inner strength and reach out for support from other people? If you don't have this inner strength and outer support you will feel very lost and empty.

Additionally, when you rely solely on one person you drain that relationship. Eventually, it will very likely become a partnership of burden and resentment. Always remember to allow others the space to find their own way in life as you discover yours. You will be doing yourself and them a huge favor. Allow growth to happen and then bring to the table what each of you learns on your own path. LEARN from each other instead of LEANING on each other for every little thing. Encourage growth instead of stifling the life you're meant to live. Diversify your emotional and spiritual wealth, and you will glow from the inside out!

Life Is the Greatest Lesson

I've sat in the classrooms, gone to the trainings, continued education, and trained some more. The outline of my learning has been necessary in carrying out the techniques in my profession, but it is my lessons in living life that have taught me the greatest lessons of all. In stepping out of the box of expectations I learned that life has its own set of rules mixed with squiggly lines. We all carve our own path while walking this earth, and it is through those steps we realize the truth of who we are, if we are willing.

It has been through my own "dark night of the soul" that I have experienced the truth of kindness and compassion toward others. If not for the risks and free-falls jumped, I would never have understood the internal anguish of the downtrodden in this world.

Welcome it. Every painful experience, every heart-wrenching difficulty, every roadblock, for it is through these tests that we discover the truth of who we are and where we are going. Your fortitude is beckoning. Allow it to reveal itself to you, to the world, and to your soul.

Fear has no place on this planet. It is simply a learned thought taught by something or someone outside of yourself. Fear constricts you, controls you, and wraps you up into a tight bud, unwilling to release. It's up to you to grab control of your soul, have a conversation with it, and follow the real you! Imagine your discoveries and you just might find the truth behind your lessons.

I Belong to Me

Let's make one thing clear. Nobody owns anybody! As soon as one thinks they own another human being they are setting themselves up for disaster. People need to feel free to experience their own pathway in life. It is not up to another person to dictate that direction. We all learn from our experiences, whether they be positive or negative. In fact, as I mentioned earlier, it is those very painful experiences that we learn the most from. If anyone thinks they need to get in the way of someone's life track they themselves will be headed down a very difficult road. Imagine feeling like you have to be one's bodyguard and follow their every move. How tiring! If you are one of these people, you know what I'm talking about. How tired are you right now? You're focusing on someone else's life instead of your own. Think of all the experiences the world is waiting to teach you on your own journey. Allow the other person theirs, even if they have to fall flat on their face! Yes, let them fall, it will be better for them in the long run. It's called lessons learned, and only growth comes from that. You will eventually see a more mature, well-rounded person.

If you are someone who is feeling controlled, you have some work cut out for you. It's going to take strength, firmness, and boundaries with the person attempting to control you. You are going to have to stand your ground and lovingly, but firmly, let the person know that you are making choices in your life, not theirs. If there is negative energy coming at you, you may envision a bubble around you to cut that energy. You are in your own personal bubble and it's just for you. Your space, your time. It is healthiest to surround yourself with people who support you unconditionally. If you have at least one or two people in your life who are there for you and listen with open ears, without judgment, you are in a good place. It's about supporting each other in being who we are and not interfering with anyone's journey. We are all on different paths in different ways. We need to celebrate our differences and embrace what each of us brings to the relationship. We are constantly learning from each other and if we can freely allow that porthole to be open we will learn and experience more in our lives than we ever imagined. Give yourself permission to fly, and allow others to fly, too!

Mental Noise

Many of us have a constant noise running through our minds, like a freight train looking for its next destination. This chatter runs longer and deeper for some, but to some extent, we all experience it. Some of us obsess to the point that it negatively effects our health physically, psychologically, and spiritually. Others may experience a milder form but still carry the tapes from their past. Are there any of you that wish for a quieter mind instead of the constant running? My guess is an absolute YES! Some of my clients experience this frustration and cry out that they just want it to stop! Personally, I can relate as I come from a family of obsessors and I drive myself crazy sometimes. It has taken much time and practice to learn to quiet my own mind, and I am here to tell you that it can be done. What does it take? It takes repetition and practice. Just like anything in life, what you nurture grows, what you starve dies. Nurturing the quiet in your mind can only lead to better health for you in all areas.

Here are some steps you can take to "untrain" your brain. When the negative thought enters your mind, immediately "change the channel" to a positive thought. For example, if you are someone who worries about getting into a car accident every time you drive your car, switch that thought. Yes, just like that, switch it! Think about what a beautiful drive you are going to have, take in the beauty around you, stay in present time, and cherish each moment of the drive. If the mental chatter enters, focus on one thing and stay with it. Think about your breathing and how your body is functioning beautifully with every breath. Notice the flowers on the side of the road, anything that brings you joy in that moment. Know that you are safe and all is in complete balance around you. If the negative chatter enters again, be okay with it and go back to your quiet focus.

Every time you practice changing your thoughts you are literally retraining your brain to think differently. Just as we can train our brains to think negatively, we can train our brains to think positively.

Are you ready now? You know what to do…breathe, focus, change your thought, and stay in the moment. Over time, you will find that this practice is a natural sedative for you. And remember, no judgment. Not of yourself, or others around you. If you fall back into old habits, pick yourself up, wipe yourself off, and get back on the slow train track. Enjoy and relax.

Peeling Back the Layers of Grey

Through the layers of grey, the root of a rose catches a glimpse of light, searching for the healing it so desperately craves. If it is able to hold the nourishment of the sun, grateful for every caress, it will survive. If not, it will sink back into darkness, losing the lesson the universe offered...

So what is all the buzz about the novel, *Fifty Shades of Grey*? I read the trilogy, and I must say, I was intrigued from beginning to end. I loved it, couldn't put it down, and from one book to the next, I traveled the deep, dark world of love and anguish with Ana and Christian. My intrigue was quite different from what the rest of the world was talking about, however. Maybe it is my therapist mind, but in my opinion, the sex was merely the superficiality of the relationship, and although it ranged from raw sex peppered with abuse to vulnerable, intimate lovemaking, the real story reaches much deeper. The obvious question presenting itself: can one who has been so severely abused in his younger years ever really know love or learn the ability to love? My answer, yes. The second part to that answer is: if, and only if, he has come to a point in his life where he truly desires change and is willing to give up his self-defeating habits to allow love in. The third piece is that this rarely happens unless he has reached a bottom so low he is willing and open to anything that will change his old patterns. It isn't unconditional love that changes the person, it is the desperate crack that opens and decides whether it is willing to receive the love that heals. People don't change people, life experience is the catalyst. If you hold that to your heart, you will be comforted in knowing that it all begins, and ends, with you. Love from another nourishes your soul, but it is you who must tend to your own garden. When you have that understanding, no one and no-thing can ever crumble your soul.

An important foundation of healing stems from the roots of humility. Anyone can talk the talk, but until you're really walking the walk, no change will occur and the beautiful rose that begins to grow within will return to its old ways, grasping on to the darkness of what it knows. Ego-driven, forgetting the opportunity Spirit offered. Living in humility, we remember where we came from, and we remember we can't do it alone. Not depending on another human to do it for us, but always knowing the universe is guiding us in perfect prose. Gratitude for THAT will stay your course.

So what about Christian Grey, you might ask? Let's remember, this is a novel, and although there are many deep truths, such as Christian's sex addiction used to escape his tormented emotions, and Ana's unconditional love putting a salve on the pain, the question remains...will Ana's love heal Christian? If Christian has reached the darkest night of his soul and has grown enough to truly desire change, yes. The future would remain to be seen.

Change is always possible. Love is always available. It is the combination of both and how one chooses to utilize it that will uncover the truth of that existence. As Neil Young so eloquently sang to us many moons ago, "Love is a rose but you better not pick it, it only grows when it's on the vine..."

Tend to your garden, the rest will all fall into place.

The Scorpion and the Frog

My sister Patty posted the fable of "The Scorpion and the Frog" recently, and it evoked a conversation that not only bonded our sisterhood but reached a deeper purpose and understanding of our authentic selves, revealing the core of who we are.

In short, the scorpion, unable to swim, needs a ride across a body of water so he asks the frog if he can ride on his back. The frog is hesitant to carry the scorpion as his instincts tell him he will get stung and they both will drown. After many promises and manipulations by the scorpion, the frog finally chooses to trust the scorpion and offers to carry him on his back. Lo and behold, halfway across the pond the scorpion stings the frog and as they're both sinking, the frog yells to the scorpion, "But you promised you wouldn't sting me, why did you do this? Now we are both going to drown!" The scorpion simply replies to the frog, "I can't help it, it's in my nature."

Some scorpions hit "bottom," learn, and choose to change. There are other scorpions, however, that never change, they simply use and abuse those with a kind heart to serve their own needs. At times, the kind are taken down with the scorpion. At other times, the kind gather their strength and move on from this toxic energy. For some scorpions, their bottom is death.

What Patty and I have come to learn about the kind-hearted is that we are who we are. Does an experience with one scorpion, or ten, change the core of our nature? Just as the scorpion's nature is what it is, so is the frog's. Do we stop our kindness with others because we've been stung or do we continue treating others with the innate love that emanates from us? With every sting, we will recognize the red flags, and possibly walk away sooner, but our nature is our nature. My belief and experience reveals the only real thing that exists in life. Love. Yes, love. Love of self and love of others. Sometimes, the best love you can give another is to walk away and allow them to learn…or not.

One thing I know for sure; those that carry light with them will always shine in the darkness. They may feel as if they're drowning, but it is simply an illusion, after all.

Reinventing Self

I had a great conversation with my oldest brother, Norm, as we walked the streets of Seattle during our family reunion. We talked about how a life worth living is a life where you never give up on reinventing yourself. A life where you tap into your creativity and explore what stirs inside; that excitement that rises when you know it is right for you, and that connection your creation has to others in your surroundings.

Reinvention is an ongoing process. Think about where you were 10 years ago compared to now. We are constantly reinventing, but the key to the process is to realize the value in reaching for your heart's desire versus settling for what you know is not working for you anymore. Is there something you've always wanted to do but fear held you back? Think about taking that first step, you may be pleasantly surprised when you do.

When I started my practice I had no idea where I was going with it. I jumped in and allowed my intellect and Spirit to guide me. One thing led to another and I learned along the way. When I started my blog, I barely knew what a blog was. I searched Wordpress and explored set up until it was done. That segued into the creation of my website. My radio show, *Help, Hope and Healing*, was planted after contacting radio stations with an idea to reach out and help others. All amazing experiences that led me in a direction to meet people traveling a similar journey. Oh, and I still want to learn to play guitar! Interestingly, that's how Norm and I got into this conversation. As an accomplished guitarist who writes his own music and lyrics, Norm was telling me how he became involved with a group named Bread and Roses, developed by Mimi Farina (sister of Joan Baez), with the idea of giving with your heart and musical talents. Musicians travel around to various facilities and connect with residents through their melodies. Norm was expressing to me, in his excited tone, how the gift of giving always bounces back. The connection and appreciation he feels with these wise older owls is overwhelming as they truly feel his music and tune in to his tunes. Both the musician and the listener have an exchange that fills them more than all the material wealth in the world. When you get this, and know this feeling, nothing can touch you. It is an island unto itself. Giving service is so important in any invention. It is a reminder that the true filling is in the giving.

What is it that you have been thinking about reinventing lately? Take that first step. Breathe in deep, eyes wide open, and GO! The learning is in the experience. You just might be surprised by what you find.

Indian Girl

MAY THE SUN

bring you new energy by day,

MAY THE MOON

softly restore you by night,

MAY THE RAIN

wash away your worries,

MAY THE BREEZE

blow new strength into your being

MAY YOU WALK

gently through the world and know

its beauty all the days of your life ~Apache Blessing

I've always felt connected to the blood and beliefs of the Native American culture. In my past-life regression, I was a little Native American girl riding her horse through the corn fields. The intensity of my mother's love created a glow that was undeniable. So much so it brought tears to my eyes. Her love filled me with a warmth I cannot describe. I sure felt it though. I believe she is with me to this day. My father was a strong, loving man who made sure we were all well cared for. Yes, this was my experience 10 years ago. It was like one of those dreams that are so real you wonder if you dreamed it or not. This is my truth.

When I landed in Santa Fe, New Mexico, 5 years ago, it felt so familiar. Surrounded by red dirt, turquoise, and brown skin, I knew I was home. As I entered the resort for my writing workshop more mementos jumped out at me. Then I entered my room, and who was on the wall but Sitting Bull! Sitting Bull is my friend's spirit guide and he has helped me through many a rough road, too. It was the exact picture that hangs in my friend's office adjacent to mine, only this one was life-size! I slept so comfortably in that room, feeling protected.

When I reach to the sky and ground myself to the earth, I am at peace. These are my spirit roots. It is my home.

Glow in the Dark

If ever you feel a negative energy surrounding you, whether it be through a person or in the environment, there is something you can do about it. Nothing. The less energy you give a negative vibe the less you feed its strength. I was talking with a friend about this experience and she looked at me and said, "Yes, glow in the dark!" I turned to her and said I loved that idea of glowing and shining your light in darkness while the energy dissipates. She began laughing and responded, "I said GO into the dark but I like the idea of glowing too!"

When we keep our light around us we surround ourselves with our protection, and at the same time, continue to send out loving thoughts to the negative energy that is invading us. That energy will eventually disappear. It will either come back with a brighter spirit or it will continue on its own way. Either way, you have created a positive energy bubble of love and light.

So the next time this happens to you, try it. Instead of fighting the energy and allowing it to grow and snowball, send it a loving kiss and huddle in your bubble. Love always wins.

The Quick-Fix Syndrome

My father used to say, "If it sounds too good to be true, it ALWAYS is!" In our age of quick-fix and immediate gratification, my father's words of wisdom have helped me stay my course. I remind my own children that it takes hard work and dedication to create anything of value. This isn't easy to do when society and the media promote having just about anything at your fingertips. It may be promoted, but it is full of false promises. Take this pill and all your problems will go away, play this game and it will fill you, let us give you money and all your debt will disappear. Too good to be true? Evidence proves the answer is yes.

Staying your course and sticking to a plan in reaching your goals isn't as grueling as some may think. In fact, my experience has been that you get there quicker than attempting various schemes that distract you from your course and having to start all over again. Keep your eye on the prize, one foot in front of the other, and focus on what it is you want to accomplish. Is it a business, starting a family, living a healthier lifestyle? A plan needs to be mapped out and followed, and it doesn't all need to happen in a day! I remind my clients that it takes patience and perseverance to truly meet their desires. If one is dealing with depression when they walk into my office, I don't immediately turn to an anti-depressant medication for healing. We work on the daily practice of self-healing first. Do some feel impatient as they work through this process? Of course, and it is all part of their learning experience. Learning patience is a skill that gives one strength to meet their needs, keeping disappointment and expectations at bay. Trusting the power of intention, and the vast universe, opens the horizon for many gifts to come your way.

Sail your ship, when the storms come gather your crew, keep your hands on the wheel, use your appropriate sails, and allow the wind to guide you. You will coast smoothly into your destination.

II.
Self-Love

The problem with co-dependency is this; when you over attach to another, with expectations of him, or her, meeting your every need, what do you have left when that person leaves you, pulls away, or simply exits this earth? No-thing.

Self-fulfillment first.

The rest will all fall into place...

Detachment as a Whole

For those of you who believe detachment is a disconnect from those around you, think again. In actuality, the opposite is true. When we detach from people, places, and things, we allow ourselves to go inward and rediscover our individual essence in connection to Source. It is this connection that creates wholeness within, preparing us for healthy exchanges in our lives, no matter what comes our way.

When one person believes they must attach to another for survival they are doing themselves a disservice. The illusion of control is a false-filler and will leave you feeling empty every time your attachment attempts independence. The healthiest of relationships develop themselves as whole individuals first and then come together, bringing to the table their unique talents and gifts. When we get tangled in between each other so much is lost in the expectations. We fall off our path, become distracted, and forget our life's purpose. Staying on track and tuning in to your spirit in connection to Source is what will bring you into wholeness. As you travel your path and flow with your authentic self, creating a balance of mind, body, spirit, and emotions, you will begin to feel a change in your soul's vibrational frequency. Old connections may fade away as new ones emerge. Any unhealthy people in your life will naturally disappear as you will have learned from that experience, choosing now to move into a different realm. All energy around you will suddenly feel "right" and conducive to your new way of living. You will feel complete as you trust your intuition and become true to yourself in every aspect of your life.

Bless everyone who has crossed your path through life for it is every experience that has brought you to your truth. Be thankful for those in your past, grateful for your present connections, and joyful for your future connections to come, vibrating side by side. Individual, whole, complete. It is then, and only then, that we all become ONE.

Self-Fulfillment First

I recently spoke with a client who was very distraught over a family situation. She states that her husband is extremely selfish, yells at their children constantly, and she continues to try to hold them all together by meeting their every need to keep the peace. Meanwhile, my client's so depleted that she's on the verge of a nervous breakdown! My first question to her was, "What have you done to fulfill yourself lately?" She has been working on this but old habits die hard, and she has been slipping back into the "savior" mode. I gave "Mother Mary" permission to go sit down. I do smile as I say this, and she knows as well as I do where her focus needs to be. Dare I say on HERSELF! Is it selfish to focus on ourselves? Women especially have a hard time with this. They are so used to nurturing everybody around them that they forget about themselves. What happens when we are depleted? Do we have anything truly of value to give out to anyone else? Are we doing our children, friends, and family any good? No, we are not. But most importantly, we are doing ourselves no good at all. In addition, when we feel responsible for everybody around us we do them a disservice. I suggested my client allow those around her to "fall on their faces" in order for them to learn their own lessons. If we jump in and save those scrapes before they cut we get in the way of the learning and healing that needs to be experienced. Those experiences are what create strength in each individual and teaches them the ability to deal with the next difficulty with grace. It is very hard to sit back and watch, especially with our own children, but in the long run all will be in a much better place.

Another important piece to this is remembering that we do not have to stand alone when we self-nurture. There is support, love, and energy beyond just us. Call it God, Spirit, the universe, our angels, whatever feeds your soul. Give in to it and ask for guidance. Meditation, prayer, and sitting in the quiet will always answer your call. It may not be in your time, but that's okay. Be patient and it will come to you. The main lesson here is to remember that you are a child of God and Spirit wishes for your happiness. Desire your own happiness. You deserve to feel joy and have your needs met. Only you can truly request this and ask for help. You are not alone, ever.

Remember to ask yourself every day, what have I done for me today? Fill yourself with all the treasures that are out there waiting for you. The more you fill yourself, the more those around you will become filled, too. The energy around you will be full of light and happiness. Soak it up. Enjoy those rays of sunshine and love every moment!

If I Am Perfect, You Will Love Me

How many of you have gotten caught in the trap of perfection as a means of getting the love you crave? Yes, I said trap. It becomes a prison and a never-ending battle that only leaves you exhausted. If it is love you are wanting in your life, I suggest you look inside to find the joy. What makes you happy? What can you include in your daily existence that brings a smile to your face? Connection to people, places, and things that are in alignment with your core values and beliefs will not only allow you to keep your spirit intact, it will allow you to fly!

When you attempt to people-please to gain approval from someone else, you become someone you're not. The authentic self is diminished and so is your self-esteem. For those of you who do this (and you know who you are), is it ever enough? Be honest with yourself. One tactic doesn't work, so you try another one. Before you know it, your self-respect gets lost and so does the respect of the person you are trying to please.

Take the chance of pleasing yourself and see what happens. The truer you are to your heart's desire the truer you are to your authentic self. Pick up your pieces and soar!

Loving Yourself

My message to you today is about loving yourself. Yes, loving who you are, who you want to be, and how you present yourself to the world. If you were brought up like I was, you were taught that "loving yourself" was conceited, it meant that you were self-centered, selfish, and uncaring. I believe quite the opposite is true. When we nurture the perfect soul we were born into we are thanking our Creator for that precious gift. We are honoring the gift of life and all that comes with it.

You are WORTH loving yourself. When you pay attention to your soul's messages of your purpose here on earth you are then able to share your gifts with others. Who are you, really? Take away all the labels you piled upon yourself. The labels of mother, employer, employee, athlete, artist, type A personality, activist...strip it all away and ponder who YOU truly are. What do you love? What creates a spark in you? A spark that allows you to shine your own individual light. A light that, if nurtured, will glow out into the world and reflect onto others. We are all meant to follow a path that leads us into the flow of all universal energy. When we are in alignment with our purpose, we do just that. All comes easily and effortlessly. Things start to show up in your life. Things start to happen, and you have no idea how you got there, but you know it feels right. You didn't control this outcome, but you certainly followed your inner guides and it led you to this point that feels aligned in all directions. The more you truly love yourself and care for yourself, the more you will experience this.

A piece of learning to love yourself is unlearning negative thought patterns that were programmed into your psyche over the years. All the rules that don't make sense and create feelings of guilt when your authentic self asks you to follow your path. Listen…listen to your inner voice and follow, guilt free, knowing it is right for you, just you.

We regain our natural state of freedom (how we enter this world) when we acknowledge the reality of the situation, without judging it, or wanting to fix it, or wanting something different. When you catch yourself in old patterns of judging yourself, move from the unconscious to the conscious. Stop, step back, and loosen yourself from the old pattern. In time, living in authenticity will become habit and you will naturally love the person you were born to be.

The Fairy-Tale Relationship

As I was chatting with a friend the other day, she blurts out, "If I could just find the right guy, everything would be fine!" "Oh, really?" I replied. We went on to discuss relationships, the stages, the expectations, and yes, fairy-tales. I finally said to her, "The fairy-tale relationship is with yourself! All other relationships fall into place after that." As children, we watched this; the good, the bad, and the ugly. In the end, the good always won and the princess and prince charming rode off on the white horse to live happily ever after. What they didn't show was the "ever after." The ups and downs, the excitement that turns mundane, the day-to-day living that becomes a schedule. But then, what kind of movie would that be? Many of us are looking for some kind of fantasy in our lives. Fairy-tales are an escape that are healthy for the imagination, but if we think life will really play out that way disappointment will present itself more often than not. As the saying goes, "Expectations lead to resentments."

So how do we live life in reality and still enjoy it to the fullest? Imagination is a wonderful thing, if we can just leave out the expectations and focus on what is healthiest for ourselves first. Find your own center in the quiet and allow Spirit to guide you. What have you always wanted to do in your life? What brings you joy? The more you can sit with yourself and enjoy your own company, the sooner you will be content in any relationship. Loving yourself first is the precursor to a peaceful, contented life.

When I think of Mae West's quote, "I used to be Snow White, then I drifted," I chuckle and think, right on! She never apologized for who she was. A woman unto herself. She'd be the first to admit she was no Snow White; never afraid to live her shadow side and experience her own journey.

The fairy-tale relationship is with yourself. Find your passion, your joy, your peace, and be mindful of what that is. Never forget YOU and all other relationships will become icing on your fairy-tale cake.

The Illusion of Control

Have you ever noticed, the more you attempt to control a person or a situation, the more it controls you? You are only fooling yourself if you think this is working for you. Anytime you set yourself up to think, "If I can just get him or her to do what I want, all will be fine," you are living the life of a co-dependent trap. In the illusion of imprisoning another you are only creating your own life behind bars. Exhausting, isn't it? By letting go and freeing others, we inadvertently free ourselves!

What is it you want from YOUR life? Adjust your focus and know that you are worth putting the time and effort into your future wants and needs. When we focus on controlling others, so much time is wasted when we could be creating our own inner pot of gold. If a situation is meant to be, or a person is meant to be in your life, it will naturally occur as you value your own purpose here on earth. The scenario you're holding on to will eventually draw closer, or drift away, as you open yourself up to your possibilities. If the drift happens, guess what? Something, someone, more in tune with you and your vibration will enter your life. Just as it's meant to be.

Learn to let go of the illusion of control and experience the delicacies flowing into your life.

Take Care, but Don't Care

If there is ever a time when you feel like you are giving too much and not getting anything in return, chances are you are! First of all, you are placing conditions on the giving which is always a losing battle. Give unconditionally with no attachment to the outcome. When we genuinely care about somebody, we want the best for them and we allow them the freedom to pick and choose how they experience their own learning. When we "care" too much and attach to the outcome, we attempt to control that person and their experience. Let go! I realize this will be very difficult for some of you. It's okay, be patient with yourself. Practice the letting go. When you want someone to choose your answer, or follow your lead, simply drop the leadline and walk the other way. Wish them well and see what happens. You will very likely not experience the power struggles you have set up for yourself in the past. You may even witness the other person come closer to you because you have given them the freedom to choose for themselves.

The other piece of taking care, but not caring, is nurturing yourself. As you place less energy on someone else's life you will open yourself up to focus on your own life, as well as the lessons needed for personal growth. Our founder of humanistic psychology, Dr. Abraham Maslow, describes this high-level need in the following way: "What a man can be, he *must* be. This need we may call self-actualization...It refers to the desire for self-fulfillment, namely, to the tendency for him to become actualized in what he is potentially. This tendency might be phrased as the desire to become more and more what one is, to become everything that one is capable of becoming."

Take care, but don't care. Take care of yourself, be loving toward others, and allow them to experience the ebb and flow of life. When a loved one falls, care and give love.

At the same time, allow them the space to gain their own strength and stand up on their own two feet. Two self-actualized people equals boundless energy!

III.
Journey to Change

So what is it that brings you happiness? Is it reaching all the "goals" you have set for yourself? Is it that house, car, career, family you so badly wanted? What then, when you attain all of those things?

Time is fleeting, happiness is found in present time, with every leaf that brushes your face and every deer that stops to look into your eyes along the road less traveled…

Notice the mysteries of life, laugh till you cry, and know that change is inevitable, with every enlightened step.

Courage

What is it you have always wanted to do but you're afraid to take that first step? What record plays in your head telling you that you cannot succeed? When we give too much credence to other people's opinions we do ourselves a disservice. No one has the power to dictate your soul's path, unless you give them permission. When you give permission you are not being true to yourself or your soul's purpose in life. Breathe deep and think deep about what it is you would go for. Take that first step and see what happens, then take another step, and another. If it is the right move for you, the energy will flow and it will soon begin to feed on itself. Doors will open and so will your heart. You will find a newfound energy to contribute to this project. If many doors close, you will have to decide if it's worth it to continue on or move in a different direction. Either way, you can stand strong knowing you had the courage to pursue something deep within you.

As you follow your path in life, there will be many challenges that appear along the way. It is your choice whether to confront these challenges or run from them. My experience has been that the learning takes place when we tackle our challenges in an emotionally healthy way. If it is something you can handle on your own, deal with it. If it is something deeper and you need professional guidance, make that call. Always keep in mind that those things you avoid along the way inevitably show up again and again. The healing takes place when you deal with it and are ready to move on. The true test begins when the challenge shows up and your choices mirror what is healthy for you versus what is detrimental.

Be courageous and choose what you know is right for you.

Ch Ch Ch Changes

Change. What is in our control and what isn't? We always have the ability to change ourselves. It is a matter of willingness, action, and surrender. Willingness to take that first step, in that first moment. Gathering the courage to step into action, pushing away fearful thoughts. Surrendering to that which is higher and more powerful than you. Trust yourself, and Spirit, that you are not only capable of change, it is a natural process in your everyday life. Create positive reminders of changes you are requesting. Put up post-it notes in your surroundings, write in your journal, create a vision board. Set your intentions and then act!

Pay attention to your physical, emotional, intellectual, and spiritual health as you set the tone. Your inner and outer balance is needed in order to gather the strength to pursue your desires. Give service to others. The more we give with compassion in our hearts, the more we fill with the love that is needed to give to ourselves. Ask for help. Open yourself up to the possibility of others entering your life to assist you. Tap in to your intuitive self and, as always, LOOK for the signs. Pay attention.

As far as changing others…I know we discussed this earlier, but I'm going to ask you again. Is it like banging your head against the wall, over and over? Plain and simple, it doesn't work! You can lead a horse to water but you know you can't make them drink. You can encourage, suggest, send love and prayers, and that is the extent of your energy you need to give. Extend your energy into what you can change, YOU! When you lead by example, those around you will eventually respond and work to change themselves, or you may move on to new surroundings more conducive to your world. The right people and events will show up at exactly the right time.

Change. Scary, exciting, needed, fruitful, and fulfilling. Put your smile on and go get it!

Healing the Child Within

Recognition of unhealthy habits opens the valve, but it is action that fosters the flow of change. This is why we all need to practice patience as we initiate change in our lives. When you consider how much time you've put into developing unhealthy habits, know that it will take time and perseverance to replace the unhealthy with the healthy. As spiritual beings living this human existence, expect that you will fall off track at times. Forgive yourself, wipe yourself off, and get back on track. In time, as you persist, the healthy will begin to outweigh the unhealthy. As you experience the feeling of positive choices you will begin to feel lighter, happier, and more joyful inside. You will begin to like YOU! As you learn to treat yourself with love and respect, you will naturally treat others in the same regard. Just remember, true change takes time. A firm foundation keeps you grounded, a quick fix keeps you stumbling.

An important piece to change is forgiveness. Forgiveness of self and others. Oftentimes, we tend to blame others for our choices. No one makes those choices but you, and until you accept this truth you will not move on. Maybe your parents didn't give you what you needed, but they gave you what they were able to give. They became parents still carrying their own baggage, and if it was packed with abuse, neglect, and personal hurts, it very likely got dumped on to you. Do you want to continue this chain, or do you want to effect change? Until you are able to let go and forgive others it will be very difficult to forgive yourself. An open heart manifests a smiling soul.

Lastly, but certainly not least, the key to all change...faith in God, Spirit, Goddess, Source, the Divine, you choose. You must believe in a power greater than yourself. The ego is a cocky entity and will knock you upside down if you invest in its false promises. When you reach only for outer fulfillment, you will often come up empty. You must reach inward to your own soul and connect with Source. Pray, meditate, ask for guidance. Go for a walk and take in the beauty of nature. Breathe in the scent of the honeysuckle on your path. Recognize the messages that come to you and follow them. Have faith that you are being guided and KNOW that you are. Gather the support of friends that carry their own truth and caring. Confide in those you trust as you work through your challenges, as we must speak from our hearts in order to heal. Never forget to give to others as they give to you, for it is in giving that we absolutely receive.

Are you ready? Let's get started…one day at a time.

IV.
Soul Connectors

"You may say I'm a dreamer, but I'm not the only one. I hope someday you'll join us. And the world will live as one." ~John Lennon

Soul to Soul

Good Vibrations!

When we begin to live in alignment with our authentic selves, the true nature of who we are, we will naturally attract situations and people into our environment that vibrate at a similar frequency. A feeling of joy, contentment, and fulfillment will show itself. The old way of living will exit into the past as you move into a place that feels like "home."

This is not to say your past experiences were a waste of time. They showed up in perfect timing, teaching you the lessons that brought you to your next level. If you were in an unhealthy relationship, stuck in a dead-end job, or just plain sick and tired, hopefully, you learned what wasn't serving your higher good and you moved on. If you chose to stay in the unhealthy, you will remain stuck until you've simply had enough. The higher road to health is always available, it is a matter of choosing to grab the rope and swing to your vibrational destination. Always your choice. Do you choose a life of positivity and joy, or a life of negativity and sadness?

Tune into your frequency and allow your karmic lessons to rise to your intended vibrational level. Open your heart, say hello to your soul family, and welcome yourself home.

Original Spirit

"Soon the child's clear eye is clouded over by ideas and opinions, preconceptions and abstractions. Simple free being becomes encrusted with the burdensome armor of the ego. Not until years later does an instinct come that a vital sense of mystery has been withdrawn. The sun glints through the pines, and the heart is pierced in a moment of beauty and strange pain, like a memory of paradise. After that day, we become seekers."
~Peter Matthiessen

When we honor and remember our Original Spirit, the child within us reunites with the light of the universe! Like a baby on her back, arms and legs swaying to the warmth of the golden sun, we recall our calming connection to Source.

The ego will pack on layers of fear, illusions of difficulties, and a handful of bravado. It is up to us to peel back the ego's armor and allow our souls to dance their tune of origination. Only then will we align just as it was intended. Free-flowing, no force, just being and falling beautifully into place along your path.

Enjoy your road, wherever you may be, and nurture nature's soul with faith, trust, love, and light…and watch…

Soul Mirror

I found some quiet, alone time late one night as I experienced *Eat, Pray, Love* at the theater. The film is very close to the book as it covers forgiveness, love, loneliness, self-soothing, letting go, fear, trust, emotional pain, and exploring your own truth.

I believe soul mates come into our lives in many different forms, at different times, when we require a particular lesson. Some remain through our lifetime, some come and go, and some we know only for a brief time. All mirrors are valuable lessons; the key is recognizing your own shadow in what your soul mate is dancing for you. Allow the joy, anger, pain, laughter, frustration, and euphoria to settle and rest with your spirit. Even when you feel lost, you are simply riding your waves to the lighthouse.

Look in the mirror. What do you see? Ahh, the unveiling of you and me.

Dream Souls

There are certain souls who telepathically connect with us on this earth

No worldly communication is needed

They come in our dreams, our thoughts, our revelations

They guide us, move us, reveal us

They are the flame to our ocean, the wind to our breath, the earth to our foundation

They get us and we get them

No words are needed

Only Love.

Who are your dream souls? Mine come in the form of spirit guides, loved ones who have passed, and friends and family living right here on earth. They are those that appear just as you are thinking of them. In earth form, it may be through a letter, an email, or a phone call. In spirit form, it may come through a dream, a special memento, or flashing lights. However your dream souls connect with you, always know that they are a piece of your connection in moving through your journey. They are reminders that you are following your path and living authentically. They are also those that will call you on it when you are not being true to yourself. At the same time, you do the same for them. Soul connectors always know.

Cherish your soul connectors. In doing so, you reach for the truth in your own soul. Every challenge, joyful run, bump in the road, and heartfelt exchange will bring you to the truth of your existence.

Soul Dance

Soul mates come in every size. Some are wise and some otherwise. They connect with intensive soul eyes...

The thing about a soul mate is they will call you on the facades you create when you get caught up in societal fantasies. They will also reign in as your biggest cheerleader, professing their faith in your ability to shine. Soul mates won't settle for less than you are, they innately know what resonates within your soul. Likewise, what you see in this soul connector they see in you, too. Soul mates come in many different forms, presenting themselves as a love partner, child, parent, sister, brother, friend, even a family pet. As your heart remains open, your soul family begins to form right here on earth.

When you're in the company of someone who you connect with at this level, your heart sings! You suddenly have the desire to reach your highest peak. You glide in that direction with ease because you know your spirit is in sync with all universal energy. It feels effortless as your dreams begin to fall into place. This is not to say the climb is easy. Our egos wrestle inside when our connector calls us on our flaws. On an unconscious level, however, we know they are right. If we are wise, we will heed their observations and follow. If we are foolish, we will ignore it and travel a much more difficult road. A connector sees in us what we are not able to see in ourselves.

A soul mate will tell you when you're not grabbing your potential, she will remind you that you're failing yourself and not flinch when she says it. She will praise your abilities more than anyone else and scratch her head, roll her eyes, and smirk at you when you don't listen to what she sees as obvious. She sees you with clarity as you put the blinders on. She grounds you, and elevates you, at the same time. She's your best friend.

A soul mate will listen to you when you throw a tantrum and then calmly look at you and ask if you are done. He holds you as you stomp your feet and wonder why the world is so unfair. He sees through to your soul and recites insights into your life at an angle you never considered. He holds your hand when you need a guide and gently pushes you when you need to take that first step. He treats you with more kindness than you treat yourself. He's your best friend.

So where are you on your soul path? Are you pushing away the sparks of light that enter your life out of fear, or are you welcoming the challenge of SEEING the purity of your soul? When you step out and bare the naked truth of yourself, that is the place where you will find honor. That is the place where you will find peace. That is where the house of your soul lives.

V.

Our Sacred Gift

"The intuitive mind is a sacred gift and the rational mind is a faithful servant. We have created a society that honors the servant and has forgotten the gift."
~Albert Einstein

Trusting Your Intuitive Self

The intuitive self. An amazing tool, if used. There are many gifts residing within each and every one of us. It's simply a matter of tapping into your inner voice. The conscious mind steers your rational, trained thoughts. The unconscious mind allows what the soul knows to come through. ALWAYS trust the soul's wisdom; it will not let you down. When a thought comes to you out of nowhere, don't ignore it. Sit with it, allow the thought to show itself and FEEL what enters. Your intuition is sharpest when your mind is quiet. Racing through your day with no meditative breaks will push away whispers from your soul. Take the time to sit in the quiet, meditate, write in your journal, or listen to soft music while sitting in the garden. Find your quiet place and allow your intuition to work its magic. It will guide you, all you have to do is listen and follow it! I have found that my intuition is at its peak when I write. The practice of tuning into my inner thoughts and living every day in spiritual practice has opened my spirit up to the universe. I am in awe of the love, kindness, and generosity that has boomeranged back to me.

Where is it that your intuition "hits" you the most? Funny enough, mine is in the shower as the water streams over me. No surprise as I am the fish, a swimmer most of my life and a Pisces. There is something about the water that calms me and allows all pathways to enter. I imagine it washes away other unwanted energy as well. Thoughts come to me when I'm riding alone in my car or sitting in my kitchen writing, as I am now. Find your place that allows your connection to Spirit to flow. Take some time out each day to tune in. Ask your inner servant to go sit down and allow your gift to overflow. Fulfillment will follow.

Silence and I

How many of you take the time to sit in complete silence? I have a little exercise for you (which may feel like a big exercise, at first). Find a comfortable chair or cushion, sit and relax into it. Breathe deep, inhaling down into your belly, allowing it to expand out and retract back in. As you are moving through each breath, simply be with the quiet for as long as you are able. No television, music, computers, cell phones, books…just you. Allow your mind to wander to whatever thoughts it holds. You will be amazed by what comes to you if you allow it, with no distractions. If your thoughts create emotional discomfort, breathe in again and ask your angels to guide you. Your intuition will become richer with this practice and will move you in directions your ego-centered mind could never imagine or create. My experience has been that when I follow a spirit-centered direction, peace surrounds every aspect of my existence. I'm then better able to make wiser decisions as I move along my journey.

If at first you are uncomfortable sitting with yourself, no worries. You are not alone in this frustration. Many of my clients have a difficult time with this exercise in the beginning. When you think of the fast-paced, instant gratification society we live in, it's no wonder. Start with two minutes and gradually work your way up. Repetition will allow you to become more comfortable sitting with your own company. The more you enjoy sitting with yourself the more you will attract like-spirited people and those that sing from the inside out!

Silence is a beautiful thing. Make a practice of embracing it, feeling the benefits of inner peace and connection to all universal energy. You may be pleasantly surprised by what may come.

When Intuition Knocks

Trusting your intuition isn't always easy. We tend to second guess ourselves when we get that "feeling." Am I really able to reach that dream? Why am I feeling like something isn't quite right? I am being told one thing and sensing something else. Always trust your intuition. It isn't something that requires forcing; simply believe in its truth. Go with your feeling; be true to yourself and the rest will all play out.

When you follow the path you know is right for you, people and projects will begin to fall at your feet. It often requires patience and perseverance so be prepared to gather your strength and travel with it. If you have a wish for your future, whether it be personal, professional, or a simple project, keep it with you. Write it down, step into it one day at a time and keep your mind and heart on your desire. Manifestation is a powerful tool. Use it and never give up. If you turn off your path it's never too late to get back on and allow the universe to work with you in reaching what is meant for you. Just remember, the more you turn off your path, the longer it will take to reach your destination. Your choice, your future.

What is your intuition telling you? LISTEN and you just might find that HEART of gold at the end of your rainbow.

VI.
Healing the Broken Heart

"The pleasure principle is the psychoanalytic concept describing people seeking pleasure and avoiding suffering (pain) in order to satisfy their biological and psychological needs. The counterpart concept, the reality principle, describes people choosing to defer gratification of a desire when circumstantial reality disallows its immediate gratification. Maturity is learning to endure the pain of deferred gratification, when reality requires it; an ego thus educated has become 'reasonable'; it no longer lets itself be governed by the pleasure principle, but obeys the reality principle, which also seeks to obtain pleasure, but pleasure which is assured through taking account of reality, even though it is pleasure postponed and diminished."
~Sigmund Freud

The Pleasure Seeker

Where is the true fulfillment in seeking constant pleasure? What is discovered over time is that it is fleeting, and in the end, leaves one with a feeling of emptiness, depression, and boredom. For the constant pleasure seeker, addictive behaviors emerge as they attempt to top their last fix. Predatory and manipulative actions take precedence as the seeker avoids the inevitable…a look in the mirror.

Any time we think we can hide from our feelings, fears, and deep, dark secrets, we are mistaken. We may run to avoid feeling the pain but we are only fooling ourselves. The pain is still there, it is simply manifesting as a pressure cooker ready to blow. When we confront our feelings, including our painful past, we are allowing the wounds to scab over and heal. Can it be an arduous process? Yes. Is it worth every tearful, angry, frustrating discovery? Yes. The only way to move through the mountain is to climb to its highest peak and back down. No short cuts. It takes work to see the light at the end of the tunnel, but remaining in the tunnel with tiny glimpses of light will only send you home with a load of inner loneliness at the end of the day.

Seek balance in your life. Pleasure is a beautiful thing, combined with self-reflection, humanity, and creativity. When we live a life of constant seeking we lose all values and decency as we search for the self-serving egotistical high. Not only are we hurting ourselves but we end up abusing others on our path to destruction. Dig deep, connect with Spirit, ask for guidance, bring meaning into your life and it will be a life worth living.

The Affliction of Addiction

Addiction is a nasty bug and once it gets its hooks in you it refuses to let go. Add in the ego, which thrives on weakness, and you have a lethal dose of insanity. As the genius Albert Einstein reminded us many moons ago, "The definition of insanity is doing the same thing over and over, expecting different results." Many people have the misconception that ego is full of confidence and direction, but it is quite the contrary. Ego is an insecure little child who wants what he wants and will stop at nothing to claim the attention that he craves. Often, attention one never received in his formative years. This starvation reaches toward outer avenues to feed the hunger. The mind trains itself (fostered by ego) to think that if I take that drink, or have sex, or eat that hot fudge sundae, or purge, all my problems will go away. Any of you stuck in this cycle know that it is, once again, a trick of the mind and a temporary fix that only gets worse and more chaotic down the road. When you wake up from your self-inflicted numbing, your problems are still there and you've only created more problems feeding your addiction. How much energy does it take to cover your tracks? How much chaos have you created along the way? How many loved ones have you hurt keeping up with your craving? How much hurt have you inflicted upon yourself? There is hope. All this energy put into feeding this monster can be redirected and geared toward healthy choices in your life.

It has been said that you remain stagnate at the age you were when you first started using your "drug." Growth cannot, and will not, occur until you get clean and mature with the tools you need to recover and claim a healthier lifestyle. The first step is admitting you have a problem. That is when humility steps up and pushes ego aside. The second step is reaching out and asking for help. There are many rehabilitation facilities and programs to assist you in staying on your course to sobriety. The third step is staying on your course, one day at a time. There is a better life for you if you take these steps and stay with it. This I can promise you. Allow Spirit to guide you, step outside of yourself, have faith and your hope will not be lost.

Below are the 12 steps followed by many programs dealing with addiction. The steps were developed by Sam Shoemaker and Bill Wilson, originally printed in the book, *Alcoholics Anonymous*, back in 1939. It has saved more lives than can be counted.

The 12 Steps

- Step 1 – We admitted we were powerless over our addiction – that our lives had become unmanageable.

- Step 2 – Came to believe that a Power greater than ourselves could restore us to sanity.

- Step 3 – Made a decision to turn our will and our lives over to the care of God as we understood God.

- Step 4 – Made a searching and fearless moral inventory of ourselves.

- Step 5 – Admitted to God, to ourselves and to another human being the exact nature of our wrongs.

- Step 6 – Were entirely ready to have God remove all these defects of character.

- Step 7 – Humbly asked God to remove our shortcomings.

- Step 8 – Made a list of all persons we had harmed, and became willing to make amends to them all.

- Step 9 – Made direct amends to such people wherever possible, except when to do so would injure them or others.

- Step 10 – Continued to take personal inventory and when we were wrong promptly admitted it.

- Step 11 – Sought through prayer and meditation to improve our conscious contact with God as we understood God, praying only for knowledge of God's will for us and the power to carry that out.

- Step 12 – Having had a spiritual awakening as the result of these steps, we tried to carry this message to other addicts, and to practice these principles in all our affairs.

The Games People Play

A client came into my office the other day, sat down, looked me in the eye and said, "I think I'm going crazy." She proceeded to tell me that her intuition and actions of her partner are telling her old habits are creeping up again. She has no solid proof that her partner is into his addiction again, but it's a feeling. She proceeds to tell me that every time she confronts him on it he gets defensive and turns it back around onto her.

When your intuition speaks, it is Spirit knocking at your door, giving you a wake-up call. Trust in your truth and allow self-care to follow. My client and I reviewed her own life lesson she is learning through this difficult time. Most importantly, she is aware that she cannot do the work for her partner or force him to make healthier choices. He has to have his own desire to change and do the work himself, just as my client needs to focus on herself and increase her strength in making healthy choices. One choice may be getting out of an unhealthy relationship. As she does her work, and begins the healing process, she will begin to feel inner peace and personal purpose. We are all capable of creating our own happiness.

Be truthful with your heart and follow the messages it gives you. When we are honest with ourselves, we honor our purpose here on earth. Nurture the precious being that you are and refuse to allow anyone to abuse your kindness.

Create your own world of joy, light, and love, and say hello to the real you.

Energy Vampires

Are there certain personalities you spend time with and when you leave them you feel depleted? Do you feel drained and begin to take on their negative energy? If you answered yes to these questions, you are very likely spending time with an "energy vampire." They are people who feel so empty within themselves that they pull from your energy in an attempt to fill themselves up. They have no consideration for others and will gladly take your energy at any opportunity. Your kindness may fill them temporarily, but they soon return for a refill before you can catch your breath, and you become the empty one! You cannot, and will not, "fix" these people and make them feel better. They have to do the internal work themselves.

So how do you keep your own energy tank full while spending time with these personalities? Boundaries, boundaries, and more boundaries! Tell them NO, guilt free. They will very likely not listen to you, and attempt to cross the boundary anyway, but you need to stand your ground. Don't answer the phone when that 10th call of the day comes in, tell them it's not a good time when they show up at your door, stop the conversation when you've been listening nonstop for hours. In severe cases, you may choose to cut these people out of your life completely. The main thing is that you set limits in order to preserve your own healthy balance.

Don't allow ANYONE to steal your peace. It is your birthright to live a life full of happiness. Embrace it!

Forget Everything and Run

"Many of us crucify ourselves between two thieves, regret for the past and fear of the future."
~Fulton Oursler

The title is a great acronym, isn't it? I've heard of it coming out of many 12-step rooms, dealing with addiction. Of course, I used the "cleaner" version, but you get the point. I'm talking about FEAR today because it appears to be so prevalent in our society, my counseling office, and everyday life. When will it be time for you to let go of your past, forgive those who have wronged you, and move on to your future fearlessly?

I will tell you when that time will come; when you can truly forgive not only those who have hurt you, but when you can forgive yourself. When you hold on to anger toward another person, or people, or situations, it's ironic how you internalize that anger, only to inflict the same hurts onto yourself and others. Until you do the work to make change, accept your part in the scenario, and look fear in its monstrous face, your lesson will never be learned and the pattern will continue in its never-ending battle. Stop in your tracks and look inward. What do you see? All the answers are hidden beneath the layers of your life. Peel back each experience fearlessly, unlearn the hurts, take control of your life, and feel the freedom it brings.

Stand up, look in the mirror, look yourself straight in the eye and ask yourself, "Is this the first day of the rest of my life?" Your choice. Your chance.

You've Gotta Get Real to Heal

Denial. Don't Even Notice I Am Lying. Another great acronym. When we repress the hurts that have happened in our lives, they continue to live inside of us. Whether you are conscious of it or not, these painful experiences will manifest their way into your life, causing more harm and roadblocks to your recovery. In order to open the pathway to healing you must face these demons. As difficult as it may appear to you, you will discover that confronting these fears only sheds light on what you need to move on. Running from your past keeps you stuck as the pattern continues over and over again.

When you are ready, reach inside and find the courage to make peace with that burning dragon. Make peace with your pain and the pain you have inflicted upon others. Yes, not dealing with your emotional challenges not only hurts you but also loved ones in your life. Uncovering all that is buried can be difficult, but in the long run it is a road worth traveling. When you discard the dead weight you make room for a beautiful garden to flourish. Only then will you be kinder to yourself and those around you.

You will know when you are ready to make these changes. Some people reach bottom before they break the earth. Some are at death's door. Some never make it. For those of you reading this who need to make changes, you know who you are. Denial or not, deep inside, you know. May you find the strength to conquer the darkness that lies within. There is a light inside of you that is yearning to shine upon you and brighten your path. Find assistance, do the work that needs to be done, and life will hold a whole new candle for you.

Let Go of My Ego!

"Edging God Out" ~Dr.Wayne Dyer

The ego. A magnificent thing. Or so it thinks. The truth is, the ego does serve its purpose. It can drive you to accomplish certain goals in life. It can also ruin you. You must use it sparingly if you are to survive with strength and grace. The thing with ego is that it likes to do battle with Spirit. One can be fooled by the enticements of the ego, promising all kinds of "fun" and power in your life, but before you know it, it has a hold on you and you're spinning out of control. You keep reaching for more, feeding it, but it is never satisfied. The empty tank is consistently empty because it is only a bottomless pit waiting for more. I've said this many times, and I will say it again, the ONLY thing that truly fills you is God, Spirit, Love. That is the purist form of emotional and spiritual nutrition that exists. You can run until you are on your knees, searching outward for that pot of gold. The pot will always turn up empty until you search inward and connect with Spirit.

Craig Hamilton, author of *Broken Open* and *A Better Life*, reveals his struggle with bipolar disorder and his clash with ego as follows: "Ego can destroy. At our most desperate point in life, our ego will not save us. It is not a building block. It is an intangible that cannot be sustained. Even though I was absolutely destroyed, a tiny spark of my ego continued to burn in the dark. After all I had been through, that granule of ego continued to resist by refusing to let me accept that I needed help. It hung on, telling me that I could still get out of my predicament. It is illogical, enmeshed with the survival instinct, and it doesn't want to let go. This was a battle that had to be fought between two opposing sides within me. Thank God, the right side won. My ego had been the agent which had refused to allow me to concede that something was seriously wrong. And, to hold that position, my ego fought almost to the very death-my death." Craig's courageous journey brought him from the depths of denial to the light of acceptance. Thank God Spirit won. Craig is here today to talk about his struggle and is helping many others through his books and his motivational speaking. In helping others he is helping himself.

Pay attention to Spirit and the messages that come to you. God is always guiding you; you need only to open your eyes, heart, and mind. Sit with yourself. Listen to the sound of the universe. Give service to others, unconditionally, with no expectations, only love. Reach inward and you will be full. You will find peace.

VII.
Letting Love In

"In these if the body will accept it, there is the meeting of self–or karmic conditions. Can it be healed? Yes, but the attitude of the body, the faith in the Divine, must not merely be assumed or proclaimed–it must be practiced in the daily life with others." ~Edgar Cayce

A Lesson in Forgiveness

True forgiveness not only involves forgiving with the mind, but it is a release from the heart that heals all wounds. We can tell ourselves over and over we must forgive, but until we work through the bridge of anger, sadness, and disappointment, we won't feel the healing within. How do we get there, you ask? Time, patience, pain, tears, anguish, turning into light, joy, enlightenment, and release. We must enter the tunnel if we are ever going to see the light. Fear not, you will emerge on the other side. More complete; healthier and whole.

The sooner we see our own reflection on our soul's journey, the sooner we will accept the experience, know it had a lesson for us, and be grateful for the strength it created in our lives. Thank those you learned to forgive, for they are the reason you have grown into the beautiful rose you have become; full of color, scents, and beauty!

When we forgive, we detach from all negative energy related to the actions of the person we are forgiving. Imagine how freeing that must feel! When we hang on to the anger/sadness/frustration we stay attached to the negative energy, and guess what? That only gives the negative actions more power as it holds you prisoner. Take your power back! Release, let go and allow positive energy to flow into your life.

When you truly let go, your mind, body, spirit, and emotions will feel lighter and full of joy and peace. Physical ailments you were feeling (and holding on to) will begin to disappear; you will feel warmth centering your heart, and your walk will have an ethereal quality. All your relationships will improve because you will feel happier within. Any negativity coming your way will deflect instead of reflect because of the light and inner peace surrounding you.

The power of forgiveness. Let go, breathe it in, and hop on the freedom train!

Two Wolves

A Cherokee Parable~

An old Cherokee chief was teaching his grandson about life...

"A fight is going on inside me," he said to the boy. "It is a terrible fight and it is between two wolves."

"One is evil – he is anger, envy, sorrow, regret, greed, arrogance, self-pity, guilt, resentment, inferiority, lies, false pride, superiority, self-doubt and ego."

"The other is good – he is joy, peace, love, hope, serenity, humility, kindness, benevolence, empathy, generosity, truth, compassion and faith."

"This same fight is going on inside you – and inside every other person too."

The grandson thought about it for a minute and then asked his grandfather, "Which wolf will win?"

The old chief simply replied, "The one you feed."

So How Do We Make Peace With Our Past?

One patient step at a time. There are a few roadblocks that get in the way of our healing. At the top of the list; impatience and fear. Our culture promotes instant gratification and if one doesn't see immediate progress they often give up. In addition, many are afraid to look at their past hurts thinking they will relive the intense pain all over again. Often, the monumental pain is created in our minds rather than the reality of facing old hurts.

Remember, old pain is exactly that. It is in the past. When we revisit it we return as a guardian rather than a lost child. As a therapist, I often will take my clients by the hand (figuratively) and guide them into the old experience. As we meet the past pain we both nurture the inner child, reminding her that the pain has served its purpose and she can now move on. The unconscious mind internalizes this process and then becomes ready for change.

We affect change by recognizing whatever difficulties we survived in our past had a purpose in creating who we are today. Through every painful act, we realized we had more strength than we imagined, our resiliency increased, we became wiser, and we developed a keener sense of intuition. All was not lost in that deep, dark tunnel; rather, if used appropriately, our light continues to shine brighter with each brave step toward healing.

Once we recognize the purpose and meaning of the "dark night of the soul," we are better able to give service and help others in their time of need. Another avenue to healing. Who knows better the compassion required in helping others than someone who has been through it? Gather your passion and use it to serve others. In time, you will realize you are serving yourself in healing as well.

Take time to meditate, sit in the quiet, allow yourself to just BE. Visualize the existence you know was meant for you. Enter a peaceful picture in your mind's eye. Notice the image before you and connect your body, mind, and soul to its essence. In time, any trauma you experienced will be replaced with healthy positivism in your life.

Continued support with a therapist, friends, and family are important in laying the foundation for healing. You will know when you are ready to fly. Take your time and think about how long it took for you to get to this place. Be patient with yourself and time. Time does heal all wounds but it is the digging that cleans out the old dirt to stave off chronic infection.

Visit that innocent child and give her a chance to live again. Peace will prevail.

VIII.
Darkness Leading to Light

"People are like stained-glass windows. They sparkle and shine when the sun is out, but when the darkness sets in, their true beauty is revealed only if there is a light from within." ~Elisabeth Kubler-Ross

Good Grief

How perfect. I'm writing this on a rainy day. A day where the sun is hiding but will show her smiling face again, after she has had her rest, after she has allowed herself to regenerate. Much like times in our own lives when we need to feel feelings of sadness, grief, or just plain exhaustion from life. Your body, spirit, and mind (conscious and unconscious) will give you signals when you need to go into the quiet and experience all that you are feeling. If we don't pay attention to these signals it will come back to bite us harder down the road. Deal with it now and your path will be paved for a brighter future.

I had a recent meeting with a client whose son passed tragically just weeks ago. None of us can really know her pain. Excruciating doesn't even begin to cut it, in my opinion. We were discussing the stages of grief, as created by Elisabeth Kubler-Ross...denial, anger, bargaining, depression, and acceptance. My client asked where she should be in her grieving. The only "right" in grieving is that you allow yourself to experience it. Pushing aside and pretending it didn't happen won't help you or loved ones in your life. This includes many types of losses in your life; a job, a relationship, moving from your home, traumatic experiences that have attempted to steal a piece of your being. The list continues. You must jump into the abyss of darkness to emerge with a lighter heart. Running away from what you must feel only accumulates a dust cloud that will keep you blinded from yourself. As I told my client, everyone grieves differently; most important is that you grieve. One may be in the stage of anger longer than depression. Some people go out of order in the stages and mix it up, while others stay right on target. Some people grieve for months, some for years. Your grieving process is your own, the main thing is that you allow it! I do recommend that as you grieve, and your wounds are open, you seek the help of a professional counselor to guide and support you. If you choose not to go that route, keep those you trust with your feelings close. Those that will listen and JUST BE there with you. One who will hold your hand through your tears. And remember, if the tears don't come, that's okay too. They will eventually if you allow the hurts to emerge. Surround yourself with those who make you feel safe. Healing will come.

Keep your light from within. Allow the rain to clear the dust. Allow love to hold you as you work through your pains. The sun will shine again.

Don't Give Up

I've always loved the song, "Don't Give Up." My favorite Peter Gabriel tune. It is a reminder that no matter what struggles you encounter in your life, there is still hope, still love that surrounds you. You only need to make the effort to open your eyes and see. Whether you struggle with mental illness, addiction, depression, or life situations that bring you down, keep your faith; reach out and call your closest friend, pastor, sponsor, therapist, sibling, or parent. Whoever it is that you know you can trust to be there for support. Accept help when it is offered, even if it is forcing that first step. It may be the first step to saving the rest of your life.

When my clients are in this state, I've heard it described as "the black hole I just can't climb out of." No matter how hard they try, they are frozen in a warped, painful time. If you have someone going through this in your life, be patient. Encourage that first step, but know that only the person suffering can take that step. This of course negates those who are suicidal and require admission to the hospital. In that case, a crisis team is required and you can call your local crisis hotline for assistance. In most cases, however, the time will come when they've reached their own bottom and they accept help. Prayer is very important during this time, asking for guidance from God, your angels, and all universal energy.

Sending many blessings and rainbows to all who think about giving up, along with their loved ones who feel pain watching their pain. My heart is with you. May you find your way.

And Then...There Was Light!

Into the tunnel, out to the light...

How many times have we heard the expression, "There's a light at the end of the tunnel?" What does this really mean? Does is mean waiting for the light, creating light, seeking light? In my therapeutic setting, my clients learn the true meaning of light as they dive into the pain. I often remind them there are no shortcuts; otherwise the lesson will be lost. No bridges to cross; otherwise the healing will pass them by. Rather, it's about digging into the darkness to come out to the other side, with a newfound awareness.

For those who wish to jump over the hump of sadness, put on a happy face, and pretend life is just fine, they will only prolong the discomfort. It often manifests in other forms, through health problems, relationship difficulties, and a feeling that you are never quite settled inside. More often than not, it sneaks up on you and hits you later in life. Embrace pain, loss, and grief as it comes and it will open up a whole new world to your existence!

So...although the urge may surge to run, all healing takes place in the process. Swim into the deep, dark ocean and watch as the light calls to you, with every heart-wrenching passage. It will be worth the voyage.

10 Tips to Push Anxiety and Depression Aside

1. Exercise. Move your body to the degree you are able; run, swim, take a brisk walk, dance, ride a bike, ride a horse, train in the gym, ski, move your arms and legs sitting in a chair.

2. Speak Up! Self-expression is crucial in the release of feelings, self-respect, and caring for yourself. The more we address the less we repress!

3. Take a yoga class. Yoga decreases blood pressure, calms your body and mind, and allows you to think more clearly.

4. Include Omega 3's in your diet. Studies have revealed Omega 3's decrease depression. In addition, a good whole foods multivitamin adds more nutrients to your diet.

5. Keep your spine in alignment. Follow up with your chiropractor. An aligned spine clears all pathways through your brain stem, allowing you to think more clearly. Not to mention, less body pain equals less depression/anxiety.

6. Meditate. Practice sitting in a quiet space at least a few minutes a day. If your mind wanders bring it back to the present as you focus on your breathing, repeating a prayer/mantra. Meditation fosters theta waves in the frontal and middle sections of the brain, thereby creating mental and physical relaxation.

7. Laugh! Laughter releases those wonderful endorphins that we experience in exercise. Watch a funny movie, reminisce about comical times with family and friends, laugh at yourself, just laugh!

8. Pay attention to good nutritional habits. Take in energy foods like green leaf veggies, fruits, and adequate proteins. Keep alcohol intake to a minimum and drink plenty of water. Become creative with smoothies. Many of us don't get enough fruits and veggies in our diet. Packing it all into one drink allows you to get a ton of nutrients in one sitting. A healthy diet gives you more energy and promotes positive thinking.

9. Give service to others. When you do it can't help but bounce back and fill you, too. There is a natural boost you receive in giving. Choose an organization, program, group, and give of your time.

10. Get your Sleep. There are a vast majority of people who are sleep deprived in our fast-paced society. Make it a point to get at least seven to eight hours of sleep a night. If you have difficulty falling asleep, take a warm bath before bed, read a book, listen to soothing music, drink chamomile tea...wind down and breathe. The more you practice steps 1-9, the easier sleep will come.

11. Okay, I'm squeezing in 11, Get a MASSAGE and pamper yourself at your favorite spa!

IX.
 *Allowing the Unknown*

"All the art of living lies in a fine mingling of letting go and holding on." ~Havelock Ellis

The Art of Living

I had an eye-opening yoga therapy session recently. So many unexpected happenings presented themselves as my therapist dug deeper into my emotions, spirit, and body. I went in with an injured frozen shoulder and came out with a warm heart. We do carry our feminine energy on our left side, which happens to be the side of my body that is aching...the ache is much more than physical pain, however, it carries a boatload of emotion, too. My boat is empty. Tapped. Giving out so much nurturing energy that I haven't taken the time to receive. My shoulder is the messenger. It is up to me to receive that message and make change.

So many emotions naturally steamed up from my heart and out of my mouth. Anger, resentments, internal control issues; leading to tears, release, and finally, laughter. I was pleasantly surprised to feel the laughter as it was quite unexpected. All the other emotions I had been feeling, but when I really looked at the situations on a deeper level, I realized just how funny life and people are. Including me!

So what did I get out of this soul search? An amazing cleansing for starters. A whole new look at situations, people, and life. And...a newfound understanding of forgiveness. We all have a part in chaos in our lives, and it's up to us to own it and observe the drama from the sidelines. It really is quite funny to watch yourself! No one is to blame for the situations you are in. All actors in the play are merely reflections of your own mirror. A glimpse into the light, dark, and gray areas of your life. Our desires and experiences complete with pains, sorrows, joys, and thrills are all available to us to discover self. Don't waste it, accept it and run with the path you're on. It's all yours to travel.

The time has come for me to receive again, and open myself up enough to trust the process, allowing the comforts in. Allowing others to give and requesting a need when it arises. Creating a balance…again. Mixed with the masculine, I am divinely feminine. I am whole.

*It has been an amazing year of healing since I originally wrote about this experience. So much can happen and enter your life in those quick 12 months. Some are conscious choices and some the universe throws you. The mixture of both have renewed my left shoulder and I am happy to report it is healed, along with the rebirth of my feminine energy! She is back in full force and ready to receive as well as give, combining the balance of my soul. I am so grateful for the healers who have helped me along this path, especially my yoga therapist, chiropractor, massage therapist, and physical therapist. I'm also grateful for my intuition for it brought me to these peaceful warriors, along with my decision to get back in the pool. Its own therapy unto itself.

It's Time to Let it Go

We've all been there, thinking we can control the outcome of someone's destiny. Trying so hard to help and hold on, but is it really helping you or the person you're trying to help? Oftentimes, we are only getting in the way of the lessons that require learning. If someone you love has a path of many falls, then you must accept that and let go of the illusion of control. In most cases, the lesson will be learned. If not, well, it was never your lesson to be responsible for in the first place. It's time to let it go...

On the flip side of this coin is YOU. Only you can steer your ship, no one else. You must be the one to pave your way, put the energy and work into your dreams, and drive to your destination. However long it takes, no matter how many mountains you must cross, stay with your own journey and you will stake your flag at the end of the marathon. This doesn't mean that you don't reach out for support along the way. Those that truly care about you will be there for you, as you are there for them. Gather support from your friends, family, loved ones, and all universal energy. You will be well on your way to your dream fulfillment.

Allow those you love to experience their own path. Release energy into your journey, let go and give Source the freedom to guide you, all the way to the finish line.

Letting Gooooo!

We all have something in our lives that requires letting go, whether it be a relationship, material items, or simple reactions to everyday difficulties. Some things take more time to release because of the perceived attachment. I suggest we are all able to let go of anything in our lives as long as we trust our inner spirit.

I had a simple reaction the other night when I came home from a lovely overnight visit with friends. I walked into the house, it looked like a bomb had gone off in the kitchen (what did I expect, it was Super Bowl Sunday), and the computer had crashed! My first reaction was a feeling of frustration and lack of control when I wanted everything in order. Well, guess what, things don't always happen as we wish so we might as well go with it when it happens! When events fall out of line it is often a message that change is needed. After my inner explosion, I reminded myself of this fact. I closed my eyes, took a few deep breaths, and asked Spirit to guide me.

Trusting your inner and outer guides is very important when practicing the art of letting go. Allow Spirit to lead when you want to control. Close your eyes, take a deep breath, pray, meditate, and ask for guidance to move forward to the place you are meant to be. No one's path is a mistake; we all have our own unique road to travel. Letting go of control is especially key when dealing with great losses in our lives. Although it is difficult to let go and feel the pain that we must experience to grow and move on, hanging on and attempting control only creates that pressure cooker that is sure to blow if not released. Often, the blow is turned inward which creates more turmoil in one's life.

So, I now sit here with my laptop, which took some work to get online. My main computer is still in crash mode, the kitchen is clean, and all is good. A little different, but all is fine in my world. A matter of perception.

As the saying goes, "Let go and let God." You will find peace.

Surrender to You

Surrendering doesn't mean giving it over to God or another entity to do the work for you. Surrendering simply means releasing control of the outcome, doing the work necessary, and allowing all universal energy to do its work. When we surrender we open up enough to accept the power of our intuitive selves to guide us in the direction that is meant for us. It may not be the direction our minds would have chosen, but in the end you will find all falls into place in a way that you could never have imagined. Created miraculously, with an outcome you never thought could have existed. It's amazing how that happens when we truly let go.

Focus on what it is you wish for in your life. Sit quietly with your intention. Release it with gratitude, do the work required, and watch it all unfold.

X.
Body and Mind

"A vigorous five-mile walk will do more good for an unhappy but otherwise healthy adult than all the medicine and psychology in the world."
~Paul Dudley White, M.D.

Move da Body! Clear Your Mind...

I often tell my clients that exercise is the best natural anti-depressant I know. How do I know this? Because I experience it in my own life. It has become such a routine for me that if I miss a day, my head and my body know it! A while back, I was having a "grouchy mom" day and my youngest daughter, Rachel, came to me and asked, "Have you exercised today mom?" I had to laugh as I looked her in the eye and said, "No, I haven't honey, you are so right on!" Out of the mouths of babes...they certainly do teach us, if we listen.

So, when you exercise what do you ENJOY doing? There's no need to make it a struggle for yourself. Do you enjoy walking, running, aerobics, hiking, biking, spinning, yoga, dance, swimming, riding your horse, skiing, or a combination of it all? Exercise shouldn't be painful, it can be challenging at times, but you should include it in your life as something that feels good. After a good walk, swim, dance class, or aerobic workout, my mind is clear and my mood improves! If you would rather stay home than go to the gym or go outside (sometimes it is weather permitting, although walks in snow storms are pretty cool), there are plenty of video workouts you can choose from.

Here is a list of some of my favorites...

Yoga; Energy Balance Yoga with Rodney Yee (Gaiam)

Power Yoga with Bryan Kest (WB)

Iron Yoga with Anthony Carillo (Goodtimes)

Pilates; Hit the Spot Pilates with Denise Austin (Lions Gate)

Tae Bo; Fat Blasting Cardio with Billy Blanks (Goodtimes)

Hip Hop; Hip Hop Abs with Shaun T. (Beachbody)

Insanity Series with Shaun T. (Beachbody) **If you're feeling insane!

Happy day everyone, and move da body ~ your head will thank you!

Nutrition Mission

We all have challenges on the balance wheel of life. My biggest challenge? Consistently eating healthy. Over the past few years, I have learned just how important nutrition is in feeding our mind, body, and spirit. If we are pumping ourselves with sugary processed foods filled with poisons, obviously all the other work we do to keep healthy will fly out the window. When we energize our bodies with green, clean whole foods, we think more clearly, increase our positive moods, and have the energy to complete those desires we've acquired through our lifetime.

As an athlete in my younger years, I never paid attention to healthy power foods. I just ate what I wanted because everyone else did. After all, I was exercising so much I could eat what I wanted, right? False. The truth is, every cell in our being reacts to every morsel we put into our mouths. Thankfully, mindful eating is a bigger topic than ever before. Science is finally backing up studies revealing the health benefits of eating more fruits, vegetables, and foods rich in proteins, providing more energy and healthy bodies. Foods high in sugar, saturated fats, and carbohydrates decrease your energy and create that nagging middle tire around your mid-section.

Here are some healthy eating habits I've learned along the way:

~ Read labels on food packages! Through my education with experts in nutrition, I look for lower grams in sugar and carbohydrates, and higher grams in protein and fiber. Speak with a nutritionist and evaluate what amount of grams are good for you. Many companies will advertise that their product is healthy, organic, and nutritional. You then read the labels and discover they are anything but healthy.

~ Do the majority of your shopping in the outer aisles of the grocery store. That is where you will find your fruits, veggies, health foods, and pretty much everything you need. Eat lots of green and colorful vegetables. Spaghetti squash is now a staple for me instead of pasta. It is delicious with spaghetti sauce, sprinkled with a bit of shredded cheese and fresh oregano. I've been experimenting with new fruits that I love. Mangos, papaya, and kiwi add a sweet taste to salads. I mix a dressing with apple cider vinegar, olive oil and seasonings to complete the fresh, appetizing meal. I cook with coconut oil and olive oil, and also use coconut oil as night cream on my face and hair. I believe, the more we intermingle with nature, the better off we are.

~ Get creative with smoothies! My daughter just made a chocolate, almond butter, almond milk, banana smoothie, and oh it was yummy! Tasted just like a milkshake but much healthier. She suggested we make a portobello mushroom burger on a whole grain bun and that would be our healthy version of a burger and milkshake. Great idea, Becca! She has become my nutritionist in many ways. My typical, everyday smoothie is packed with dark leafy greens (kale, spinach, or collard greens) along with fruits, chia seeds, flax seed, goji berries, almond milk, coconut water, ice, and water. Mix it up to your liking and enjoy!

~ For snacking I have a great mix of raw almonds, unsweetened coconut flakes, dried cranberries, and sometimes I add cacao nibs for a little chocolate flavor. A small handful is very filling and satisfying. I'll also snack on a piece of fruit or healthy protein bar (always good when you can SEE all the ingredients in the bar, be sure to read the labels). The name of my favorite bar is Kind.

~ Drink plenty of water and add fresh lemon as often as possible. Lemon alkalizes the body, once again, creating a healthy balance.

Awareness in nutrition is the key to rounding out your balance wheel in life. If it is missing, you will not function to your optimum level. Make it a practice in your daily living; your mind, body, and spirit will thank you.

Body Break!

Among the quick movement of the world, I'm noticing more and more exhaustion rolling around me. People are running through life and spinning so fast that they aren't able to breathe, center, and connect to the nourishment of Source. When we listen to the signals our bodies give us, there is a high probability we are preventing illness, injury, inefficiency, poor decision-making, and poor performance. When your body speaks, listen!

How does your body speak to you when it is depleted? You walk around tired all day. Your extremities actually tingle with exhaustion and your muscles ache. Your memory is impaired. You're irritable and have less patience with others. You feel depressed, angry, sullen. When we love ourselves enough to administer self-care, we are feeding the temple that carries us. Pay attention!

Sleep when your body cries for rest. Meditate when it screams for calm. Rest when it can't carry you anymore. Replenish the emptiness within and you will accomplish what is needed in your life with ease. When you are exhausted, every movement is an effort; rested, and life flows effortlessly.

Treat yourself with the love, care, and nurturing you deserve. You are porcelain walking this earth. Protect your beauty within and you will never be without.

R-elax
E-xhale
S-leep
T-une out!

Reach for the Orange!

Especially during the holidays, where the candy and cookies abound, it is important to keep your eye on the prize. The prize being you, of course. What goes through your mind when you start to reach for that cookie when you've already had two or three or four...? You know it's not healthy for your body to consistently overindulge, so when you reach for that sugary substance pay attention to your thoughts. Are you not feeling okay with yourself today? Are you trying to fill yourself with food instead of doing the inner work you know sustains you? Whenever we depend on an outer substance to fill us, we experience a false sense of wholeness. Think about it; you eat, drink, ingest the false-filler, you tell yourself this feels great, then you come down and you don't feel so good. It's not really your friend, it only pretends to be...to hook you. If you don't pay attention and love your body and yourself enough it will be the one eating you!

So...I suggest you reach for the orange! The orange being the metaphor for many healthy ingredients we can happily put into our bodies. This is not to say that we shouldn't treat ourselves to sweets on occasion, but you know when too much is too much. Be honest with yourself. Listen to your mind and your body. Are you jiggling more than you like when you run down those stairs? Been there! Are you more lethargic during the day? Been there! Are you more irritable? Been there, too! We constantly get messages from our body, spirit, and mind...pay attention and nurture you. If you treat your body like a temple, it will shine from your heart, soul, and mind!

The Body Epidemic

It's an epidemic that has swept through millions of girls and boys, and men and women in our culture. The mind's illusion believing the myth, "If I am thin enough, hot enough, muscle-cut enough, beautiful enough, then I will get everything and everyone I want and my life will be perfect." Quite the opposite is true as society preys on people's vulnerabilities. It is the insecurity of the mind that feeds the ego, believing in these false-fillers.

Men and women alike sell their bodies through starvation and over exertion, creating a false sense of self that screams for attention. When the fearful ego attaches, scenarios of people using and abusing one another ensues. Those with the illusion of perfection through their bodies often feel entitled and expect others to support them financially, physically, and emotionally merely because of their outer facade. At the same time, those supporting those with this outer appearance have their own expectations leading to a lack of respect and conditions placed upon the relationship. It is a shallow existence with few rewards, leaving one feeling empty and full of emotional and spiritual pain. This lifestyle feeds the "Fat Cats" of the industry, leaving the abused feeling useless, hopeless, and helpless; often leading to other addictions to fill the void. A vicious, insidious, sad cycle.

When will we stop focusing on the deception of perfection and begin to take interest in what truly fills our mind, body, and soul? Today would be a good day to sit amidst the flowers and discover the substance of your authentic self. Simple and true.

Sing Me a Lullaby

"Sleep is the best meditation." ~Dalai Lama

When we consider the whole umbrella of healthy living, we think about nutrition, exercise, emotional expression, spiritual growth, along with many other aspects, but do we consider the amount of sleep we get? Sleep is a crucial piece that is needed in order to maximize the benefits of all of the above. If you do not feel rested in your mind and body it rejects all lines of learning. Think about this, when you feel rested your mind is keen and your body is energized, ready to give and receive more energy. You need to fill your own tank in order to reap the benefits of life.

Wayne Dyer has said that five minutes of meditation is like seven hours of sleep for him. He is a master! I meditated for 15 minutes yesterday as the sun shone on me, providing more energy. I absolutely felt more vibrant and alive throughout the day. I also know that I need a good night's sleep. A few hours doesn't cut it for me. When I meditate or rest for about an hour that does revive me, but let's also look at prevention. Here are some steps that have helped me get a good night's sleep:

~Take a warm bath or shower before bed.

~Read a book.

~Listen to guided imagery/relaxation as you lay in your bed.

~Take a melatonin supplement.

~No caffeine or alcohol five hours before bedtime.

~Wind down with calming activities.

~Exercise during the day, no exercise just before bedtime.

~Meditate during the day.

~Express yourself emotionally and spiritually throughout your day.

~Journal your thoughts and feelings.

~Eat healthy with lots of fruits, veggies, water, and proteins.

~Sleep with no light in your room, or very little, if you need light.

~Drink a sleepy tea like chamomile before bed.

Happy slumbers, all. Remember, replenish, give to yourself and others, and replenish again. Always fill your tank. Rest will come naturally the more you love and care for yourself. Wishing you all a salubrious day!

At First They Will Ask You

At first they will ask you why you're doing it, then they'll ask you *how* you did it. I initially heard this expression while I was dedicated to becoming more fit and eating healthier. In the process, I lost some weight and became leaner. Those who were comfortable in their own mind and body were very supportive and appeared genuinely happy for me. Those who were not had a difficult time with my changes. Remember this, when someone has an issue with your journey it is more about them and less about you. Anyone who is comfortable in their own skin is happy for you when you attempt to become comfortable in yours. Subconsciously, and sometimes consciously, people project their insecurities onto you and feel fearful when they sense change. Do not allow them to take you off your course. Tune in to what feels right for you, stay strong and keep on traveling. If they are true friends, they will come around, if not, they will move on. Stay true to you and you will attract those meeting you at your vibrational level.

When your genuine friends stick around, don't be surprised if they eventually ask you how you did it. This is a sweet validation, not only for you, but a connection with your friends in living healthier lives.

Always be true blue to you and you'll begin to experience the win/win scenarios of life!

XI.
In My Life

What better place than the heart of my book to include the many loves in my life? I debated adding this section because, well, it's all about me. I chuckled and reminded myself that sharing my experiences, and revealing some of my personal life, will simply show my own vulnerability and allow a deeper connection with my readers. No doubt, I display my vulnerability and experiences throughout the book, but this section goes a bit deeper, revealing my personal life, friends, and family. In my life, I've loved them all.

Peace Begins Within

Peace starts within each one of us. When we have inner peace we can be at peace with those around us."
~Dalai Lama

A dear friend of mine sent me this quote from the Dalai Lama the other day. We were talking about how holiday time can be stressful for many families as it brings up a multitude of emotions. There are numerous expectations set around the holidays; the "supposed to's" of who gathers where, who's getting along with whom, and the comfort level of the family dynamics.

When we take the time to go inward, and tap into our own peaceful place, the world around us settles quietly, like the early morning snow on a sturdy spruce. True peace can only be felt when our hearts open to loving ourselves and those around us. I learned this lesson of love from my father early on in my life. There were certainly many times he could have thrown his arms up in frustration with his eight kids, and walked away, but he never did. Instead, he chose a peaceful stance, never judged, and waited. He might not have agreed with our choices, but he chose to stand by with a quiet strength. Of course there were trials and difficulties, just imagine growing up with five brothers and two sisters in the '60s and '70s, but my parents always backed each other up when it came to dealing with all of us. And in the end…Love Stood.

Following is a photo of my parents that has been floating around my family this holiday season. This is where it all began…and then there were 10!

Wishing you all love and peace in your hearts today and always. When we get caught up in the illusion of what it is we're dealing with, remember, peace is only a heartbeat away…

Pat and Norm on their wedding day, August 23, 1947

Sedona Serenity

Glorious Sedona

My sisters and I embarked upon an adventure that will always be treasured in my heart. My sister Patty had seen a shaman named Clay Miller on OWN (Oprah Winfrey Network) with Sarah Ferguson. She was very intrigued and it hit a spot in Patty's soul that pushed her to call me and excitedly say, "We have got to see this guy!" While we were on the phone, I looked him up online, found his website, and agreed it was a must. The Native American feel of Clay drew me to him even more. We contacted our sister, Mary, and after a few emails back and forth, the three of us had an appointment to see Clay. Just like that.

February of 2012 will forever be archived in my soul. Not only did we have the pleasure of meeting with Clay, he happened to live in one of the spiritual mecca's of the world ~ Sedona, Arizona. I had visited Sedona before, and felt a deep connection, but this visit, well ~ I will do my best to match my kaleidoscope of feelings with my words.

The first full day of our arrival was our meeting with Clay. We drove up into the beautiful mountains of Sedona, nature beckoning us as we climbed higher. Pulling into Clay's driveway, three friendly dogs came out to greet us, followed by Clay. He had a very relaxed manner about him, outlined by his long silver hair braided in pigtails. I immediately felt comfortable in his presence, and I could sense my sisters did too. He and his four-legged beauties welcomed us and guided us into their home. We all sat on the floor surrounded by pillows, "Tupelo Honey" playing in the background, and then we began.

Clay described his role as letting go and allowing Spirit to move through his voice, remaining present as an open vessel. Mary, Patty, and I then laid down in a circle on our backs, our heads nearly touching each other, creating our own human star. Closing our eyes, we took in the energy of the room, and Clay began. He came to me first, lightly touched my stomach and voiced every emotion I had been feeling for the past few years of my life. He saw me, felt me, and spoke my voice with a clarity my mind could never muster. The energy that moved through him, direct to me, had tears streaming down my cheek bones deep into my heart. I began to express softly, then a bit louder, then louder and louder, until all energy inside of me was released. I was dancing freely under the night sky, feeling the moon and the stars as I twirled in delight. Finally, my external vision mirrored my internal feelings, creating wholeness in my soul. Clay then moved on to Patty, then Mary, and as he did, I felt as intensely emotional hearing their scenarios as I did mine. The three of us crying in unison. The fact that we are sisters, I'm sure, made the experience even that much more powerful. After we said our goodbyes to Clay, and started down the driveway, I don't believe our feet touched the ground. We drove back to the hotel in silence.

Fast-forward a couple of days and now enters a complete in-body experience. Life is, after all, all about balance. I say that with a chuckle under my breath. You will understand as this story unfolds. So, after coming down to earth since our day with Clay, we went on some amazing hikes, enjoyed a massage, and visited The Chapel of the Holy Cross. All beauteous. We then decided to go out for some pizza and enjoy a band. While we were eating our pizza, we met some nice natives and chatted a bit. As we were leaving, they warned us to be careful on the roads as the police were out in full force. We laughed and said, "Yeah, yeah, okay, we're just going down the road to see a local band." We thoroughly enjoyed the band, and a good time was had by all. On the way back to the hotel, lead-foot Mary was behind the wheel, but only going a few miles over the speed limit. Well, you can guess what happened next, the flashing rabbit ears were glowing through every window in our car. Before we know it, we're pulled over and a police officer walks up to Mary's window and says, "I'm officer Peyote, your license and registration, please." I'm thinking, seriously? Are you kidding me? We get pulled over in the middle of the desert and now officer *Peyote* wants to see her license?! I don't know what kept me from bursting into a thunderous roar right then and there. Mary, who might as well have been called Virgin Mary in our family, never got into trouble for anything. She was known as sweet, quiet Mary, the Saint. The next thing we know, officer Peyote asks Saint Mary to step out of the car and promptly handcuffs her. That was it for me, Patty and I both jumped out of the car, out of instinct, to protect our sister. Quick as a flash, we have three officers in our faces, hands on their holsters, yelling at us to get back in the car! This was all so surreal. Mary was whisked off to jail and Patty and I were left scrambling for legal help.

To no avail, everyone we called was either on the east coast (and it was in the middle of the night), or we were out of luck with every number we contacted. After calling the jail, they told us we had 10 minutes to find an attorney or Mary was spending the night in jail. Our time was up. We felt helpless, life as we knew it had turned upside down at the flip of a siren switch. Just as we felt defeated, baffled, and frustrated by the injustice of it all, a knock comes to our door. We open it and there is Saint Mary looking at us with her sweet smile. Our mouths wide open, unable to speak, we finally mutter, "What happened?!" She simply said, with a twinkle in her eye, "They were looking for a nun on the run."

LEFT: Patty and Mary contemplating between the red rocks on one of our gorgeous nature hikes. ~ RIGHT: Patty and me hanging at the Hopi Rock after our relaxing lunch at the beauteous Enchantment Resort.

Circle of Friends

"The only way to have a friend is to be one."
~Ralph Waldo Emerson

I am so very blessed to have amazing friends in my life! Some I have known a lifetime, some are more recent, and some have re-entered. For whatever reason, they have connected to me in a beautifully spiritual, and often serendipitous, way. My heart fills when I think about how their love has carried me through so much in my life, as my love has surrounded them too. A true friend is one who loves you unconditionally. No judgment, no expectations, just pure love. They are the ones who are always there for you, no matter what. Friendships are give and take, and it is important to remember the giving part. It all circles around and grows with each passage of trust.

My chain of girlfriends began the day I was born. A picture of me and my babysitter sits on my mantle. I was two and she was just a teenager. She is still a member of our family to this day, I call her mama sis. She is so very special to all of us. My sisters have been there for me through thick and thin, as I have been for them. We're sisters, a bond that never breaks and a love that never fades. My dear childhood friend who has been so full of unconditional love since I can remember, unbelievable the heart she has. My Round Robin girls, we've been through so much together. We started our Round Robin chain letters 30 years ago and it continues today, including memorable reunion trips. My forever "roomie," our intuitive connection never ceases to amaze me. We were assigned as roommates our first day of college and hit it off immediately. We remained together all four years and we continue to build more memories, including collaborating on this book. My college swim team co-captain, who provided so much fun and support in our swimming days, and remains a wonderful friend today. My silly friend who hikes with me and takes me up the crazy hills of Horseheads. Always a laugh, and I continually feel renewed after our time together. My dear friend who has the spiritual wisdom, patience, strength, and kindness that truly amazes me. A bond that was formed many years ago as Spirit brought us together. My sweet soul sister who is full of so much love, grace, and compassion, it's unfathomable the light she emits. My latest wonderful spirit connection who gives so much love and always reminds me of the importance of the spirit of the horse. All my sister-in-laws who continue to be so special to me and provide a spectrum of beautiful colors to our family. So many friends along the way, too numerous to mention, but I know I am beyond blessed to have had each of them touching my life.

Always remember your circle of friends and how their love has weaved through your life. I don't know where I would be today without the love of friends surrounding me. As I carve my way, they have helped shape me into the spiritual being I have become. Thank you, friends. From the bottom to the top of my heart, I LOVE YOU!

I Love You, Dad

January 25th

Today is my father's birthday. He left this earth to fly with the angels 20 years ago. The thing is, my dad was an angel on this earth. For those of you who knew him, you know what I mean. I cry as I write this, thinking of so many memories. He was a guy who was always there when you needed him. Not only was he a father of eight children, he took some others under his wing as well. Always the dad with the stop watch at the swim meets, always on time to pick us up at the club, always the one you could depend on, literally the glue of our family. The sound of his whistle is so clear to me right now, sitting here in silence. As my brother, Norm, wrote in one of his songs..."And I can smell the lilacs bloomin' in the springtime sun...and I can taste the McIntosh Apples when the harvest comes...and I can still hear my daddy's whistle a mile down the road...just this feeling I have right now, makes me wanna go...oh down...old Brayley Road...the country in my soul...how I loved those days...on old Brayley Road."

My dad left me a dime last night. It is one of the many ways he lets me know he's still with me. I find them in various conspicuous places. It gives me comfort to know I can talk to him at any time, night or day. He especially shows his presence around his birthday, and Valentine's Day, the day before he passed. So fitting for such a sweetheart. I love you, Dad.

Remember those you love, today and always. They are treasures that may move to another dimension, but they can never be lost.

DAD

There was a man, and he was tall and strong
And he ran right through my life.
He was sharp and funny, but he was quiet
most of the time.
And he is the eagle in my soul,
He carried me over my doubts, there in the
rain he washed them out...
And into the sun he lets them fly,
Knowing that love will never die.
And I saw him running once, and with his
hair blowin' in the wind,
He seemed to me to be the greatest man that
ever lived.
And I wonder, as I think of him, and a tear
drop fills my eye,
Does he know, that love of his, still runs
right through my life...

Song by Norm Weintraub, Jr. (my bro)

Dad playing on one of his fishing trips with my brothers ~ Parry Sound, Ontario.

I Will

"Success is not final, failure is not fatal: it is the courage to continue that counts." ~Winston Churchill

Recently, I did something I thought had passed me by. It's an endeavor I often pondered about, but with the busyness of life and the little questions in the back of my mind, I convinced myself I had done my time. I was wrong. All the fear I accumulated over time was nothing but a cavern of deception. So I pulled together my best suit, cap, and goggles, and joined a Masters Swim Team. As a competitive swimmer from the age of 5 to 22, I wasn't sure I could pull this 51-year-old body together enough to swim a practice beginning to end. I was pleasantly surprised when I touched the wall at the end of my 100th length. Not only did I feel an accomplishment, I felt like I had returned home.

Anything we do in life never has to end. If it's something that has brought you joy in the past there's no reason why it can't be added to your present. Often, I ask my clients what they do for themselves that brings them happiness. More often than not, the answer is, "I don't know." That's when I direct them to reach deep down into their bellies and recall what they loved or dreamed of as a child. That's when their face lights up and they begin to remember all they have shoved down to meet the needs of others. Given the choice to rediscover your successes in life, what courageous journey would you embark upon?

I know many, and I will. Allow your heart to search, you will, too.

Fresh out of the pool after my 50 yard butterfly race at a
Masters Swim Meet in Skaneateles, New York.
Photograph by Louise Cady Fernandes.

A Blast from the Past!

Well, I did it. I ventured in to my first Masters Swim Meet, and what a wondrous experience it was! The fact that it was at my alma mater, Ithaca College, made it even sweeter. The last time I swam in an IC pool was 30 short years ago, and needless to say, the old pool is no longer there. In its place is a brand new state-of-the-art swimming facility, equipped with an Olympic size pool, swim tank, and huge hot tub. Nostalgia hit me big time as I read the records of the IC Bombers on the wall. I might have been up there for a minute back in 1980. It warmed my heart to think back; and if I quiet my mind long enough, looking far into the bleachers, I think I might have seen my dad with his old two-hand stopwatch yelling out my split times. Oh, the good old days.

The biggest difference I noticed with Masters Swimming compared to college swimming is it's so much more fun! All the pressure is off and it's more about doing your best rather than having to beat the person next to you. Since you're swimming alongside women and men of all ages, shapes, and sizes, according to your qualifying time, you don't know where you're going to place in your gender and age group, until the end. My end resulted in two firsts and a second in my age group. Pretty sweet for a first meet. I very likely had the biggest smile on my face mixed with shock and wonderment while I stood at the scoreboard. Sometimes, it's the little things that bring the biggest feelings.

I'm so grateful for my friend, Louise, who has been encouraging me to take the plunge for two years now, around the time she started with her Masters Swim Team. She had expressed to me how much joy she felt swimming again, but it wasn't until I felt the flow of practice, and excitement of the meet, mixed with the memories of what's in my blood, that I really got it. And a huge added perk, she will be joining me next month at my next meet. My bestie high school friend, and swim team co-captain, swimming together once again. What could be better than that?! Perhaps a weekend at my cottage intermingled with hikes and savory dinners, pre-swim meet. Oh, life is good.

Old swim pals ~ me and Louise at the Skaneateles Masters Swim Meet, February, 2013

What Your Soul Knows to be True

May, 2013

Well, here we are, another spring upon us and it feels like life is coming alive again! Not sure how many long northeast winters will be in my future. The timeline of life travels so quickly and there's much to be enjoyed along this pristine and dusty road stretching ahead of us. My oldest daughter, Kelley, ventured out to California and is returning soon, and now my second daughter, Becca, is wanting to check out schools in Cali. As Joni sings, "California, oh California, I'm comin' home..." I've always related to that song but whoever knows where I'll land. I sure don't. Santa Fe felt like home to me, too. As soon as I touched down at the airport I felt it. The pull of red dirt, turquoise, and silver tugged at my heart. Why? I don't know, but in some ways I do. My point of this reminiscent writing is to follow your heart's desire. Don't put it off, the time is now, and whatever you do, live in the now and enjoy every moment as much as you possibly can.

My latest endeavor? Embarking on a race called Hero Rush, created by our heroic firefighters. It's a 5-mile, 18-obstacle course consisting of freezing water, tube tunnels, fire hose carrying, rope climbing, smoke house running, tire trekking, fire hopping, and more. Some people think I'm crazy and ask why I would do such a thing. I think to myself, why wouldn't I? I get comments like, "You're 52, don't you think you should settle down?" or, "Aren't you worried about getting hurt?" or, my favorite fear comment, "Oh my, that looks so hard, are you sure you can do it?" These comments don't stop me, they just challenge me more. This is what I know to be true, I won't "settle down" until I take my last breath. And then the world of Spirit opens up along with a whole new playground full of love, learning, and experiences. Except this time, it's played out with complete unconditional love beckoning behind the veil.

Always trust what your soul knows to be true. Listen for the signals and see the signs. Our connection to Spirit is so very strong, we need only to practice awareness. My truth? The familiar red dirt, turquoise and silver points me to my inner knowing. I trust it, and I know why. This fair-skinned, blonde-haired girl with green eyes will always be a Native American girl at heart, riding her horse through the corn fields.

The Act of Balance

I did it! I ran through Hero Rush (my 5-mile, 18-obstacle course) after days of rain and mud up to our ankles, and oh what a rush it was! Our team photo revealed the excitement we were all feeling before the race, and to be honest, my excitement was mixed with nerves as I had no idea what I was in for. As it turns out, it was one big wet muddy blast! *Psychology Today* recently published an article about people who are consistently curious and present challenges in their lives as happier than those who remain complacent. All I can say is that I felt ecstatic for days after this last curious challenge for many reasons. I pushed my body to reach to the outer limits, I laughed a boatload as we slipped through the muddy ravines, and most of all, I felt joy in my heart. When the race was over, and they pulled out the last hose to wash us all down, I danced through the water with a smile on my face and a light in my soul. Yes, I was a giddy girl.

With that being said, some recent events have forced me to remember the importance of balance in our lives. My high wire slide on obstacle number 15 may be an example of a physical balancing act, but life, well, it's one great big act of balance. We must choose what is to be a priority at any given moment. Sometimes, it won't be what you planned but it will be what you know in your soul is right. Just a few days ago, we lost our beloved family dog, Ollie, and on the heels of that, my mother was in need of increased care in her assisted living facility. Between grieving and caring for my mom, certain things have to take their place on the back burner. I have a swim meet coming up, which I should be training for, but more important things happened to pop up on my priority scale. After spending hours with my mom and organizing changes for her, I was just getting ready to leave and head to swim practice when her nurse's aide walked in the room and reported that mom had a last minute doctor's appointment. Her aide offered to take her but I knew in my heart the right thing was for me to take her. In setting my outer goals aside (and missing swim practice), I nurtured my inner sanctum by aligning with love. Not to be a martyr, simply to listen to the silence of my soul and believe in my knowing. It turned out to be a great day with mom, ending with a lovely lunch in her room. She will be 86 years young this year, and I must say, it's been a life well lived. A woman who was extremely curious and challenged herself constantly.

And so it goes, I have my swim meet next week. Am I physically prepared to swim my best? Nope. Am I okay with that? Yep. There's so much in life to love and be grateful for. Trophies and accolades are nice but the icing on the cake is giving and feeling the love that surrounds. I plan on having a great weekend with my high school swimming bestie, Louise. We don't take swimming as seriously as we did in high school but we sure have a ton of fun with it. I'm certain it will be a wonder~full weekend at her lake house this time, enjoying the views of New Hampshire, sipping a little wine, reminiscing and laughing. Lots of laughs.

**My physical act of balance in Hero Rush.
Photograph by Capstone Photography.**

**Horses were always Mom's great act of curiosity.
Here she is on Noble Savage in 1966.**

Shifting Sands

Mike strolling our Cayuga Lake beach with Jazzy and Ollie
~ the heavens validating their soul connection.

Amazing how life can shift in just three short weeks. From expectant loss, to tragic loss, to new birth. Below are three short paragraphs describing the gamut of emotions I experienced during the month of July, 2013. Just like that, life can change and bring you excruciating sadness turning to joy and light. The sands settled on my heart and opened a whole new world for my eyes to see. Never forgetting the light that remains, and simultaneously, opening my heart to new light.

Our dear, sweet Ollie flew into the heavens recently. We all circled around him and gave him our last round of love ~ including Jazzy who snuggled in with us. Those of you who knew Ollie know what a big gentle soul he was. He gave us 12 years of big love; from pony rides (when Rachel was a baby) to big bear hugs (to warm us) to majestic protector (literally coming toe to toe with black bear in our backyard). We will forever miss you, Ollie Bear, always in our hearts.

It is said; when two souls are deeply connected and one exits this earth, the other is sure to follow. Our sweet soul, Jazzy, followed her love companion, Ollie, soon after we lost our big gentle bear. We were expecting it with Ollie, as he was ill for some time, but Jazz, it came out of the blue. Just two short weeks after losing Ollie, Jazz let us know it was time to join him. I should have known when she nuzzled him nose to nose as we circled around him to give our last round of love. They came to us as pups 12 short years ago, and now their souls will live together forever. We miss you my angel girl, always full of love and loyalty. Always with kindness in your heart. Always my soul connector. Fly high with Ollie and shine your angel wings around us. You are both forever in our hearts.

Well, I thought it was too soon for a little one to enter our lives after losing Jazz and Ollie, but my daughter, Rachel, was persistent and I caved. So happy that I did because little Jude has brought back that spark that diminished when Jazz and Ollie left. I feel them with us more than ever ~ in every hug, every smile, and especially when I see Luke and Jude romping together. The love continues to expand.

I suppose it's no surprise that I've had so many animals come and go in my life. I grew up on a farm and my husband, Mike, is a veterinarian. We were very fortunate to be able to say goodbye to Ollie in the comfort of our home. Our circle of love consisted of me, Mike, and our three girls; Kelley, Becca, and Rachel...and then Jazzy snuggled in. They know, don't they? Our animals feel more than we think they're aware of. Spiritually, I believe they're much more in tune than the human race...that is, until we strip away those layers of conditional life. I have been blessed with a plethora of animal souls streaming through my life.

There is no doubt, when I move into the spirit world, it will provide peace, love, warmth, and yes, a boatload of four-legged loves.

LEFT Majestic Ollie Bear ~ CENTER: Rachel and Jazzy enjoying some quiet fishing time on Cayuga Lake. ~ RIGHT: Becca loving our new baby Jude. Captured by Kelley's beautiful photography.

Goddess of the Dawn

My glory days with Early Aurora, circa 1971.

I would be remiss if I didn't include the special bond I had with one very special girl; my horse, Early Aurora. In Roman mythology, the meaning of Aurora is "goddess of the dawn," and oh what a goddess she was! A bright light shining into the dim of the morning. She was my guiding light, my maternal protector, my soul mate. She safely carried me through trails, over hurdles, and around arenas from the time I was 10 years young to the ripe old age of 13. Soon after, her time came to retire on our farm, soaking up the leisure life of pastures and blues skies, until she passed through the veil, shortly after retirement.

Aurora has been shining her bright light on me, yet again, as of late. Forty-three years after she came to me, another shining light tapped on my soul. Aurora's previous rider/soul connector found me on Facebook and asked, "Are you by chance the Cindy Weintraub who rode Early

Aurora?" I replied, "Yes, she was very special to me. Who did you ride with?" When she told me she was Aurora's previous owner, my body quivered in chills. She had kept a Christmas card I sent her those four decades ago when Aurora came to me. A photo of Aurora and me, and my name, enclosed. Immediately, I felt bonded with this person who I knew loved Aurora as much as I did, and our connection has only grown since then. Barb has become such a sweet soul sister to me, and, of course, we have more in common than I ever would have imagined. The bond we have, it all makes sense to me now. At 61 years young, she runs, swims, moves through nature walks, eats very healthy, and has more energy than a 15-year-old. Our spiritual beliefs are so in sync it leaves no doubt that Aurora's spirit not only arranged our recent connection, but the passing of Aurora's light from Barb to me those many dawns ago. Barb is now a bright light in my life, with Angel Aurora in the middle.

The grace of meeting Barb was not only enlightening but cathartic in my own healing. As I was in the shower one morning, where most of my profound intuitive thoughts come to me, I realized the real reason I quit riding while I was so young. My excuse was that I wanted a social life with kids my age (and part of that was true), but the deeper meaning expressed itself through my stream of tears, washed away by the shower cascade. You see, Aurora retired young because she had cancer. I realized that morning, surrounded by the ease of water, that I blocked the pain of losing Aurora so deeply that I quit doing something I loved. At such a young age, I didn't know the value of grieving and moved on, hiding the hurts festering inside. For those of you who can relate, you know the bond between a girl and her horse. It's stronger than many friendships throughout a lifetime. I am so very grateful for Barb entering my life, for she not only gave me the gift of a beautiful friendship, She unknowingly pushed me to feel the pain and grieve my long lost love. Not only Aurora, but the joys of riding itself. I know Aurora sent a spark through both of our hearts, creating a bond forever connected to her spirit.

When painful times come upon you, remember, "This too shall pass." Spirit has given us the blessing of amnesia when it comes to pain. Allow yourself to feel and express, especially when you think you can't feel anymore. The nights will eventually give way to the glory of the dawn.

LEFT: Barb and Early Aurora shining their light. ~ RIGHT: Aurora and I were both 10 years old in this photo. I remember this moment like it was yesterday. One word. Joy!

XII.
Spirit Song

There are many beautiful views I run into on my walks. Sometimes, a deer may cross my path or stop and stare at me, delivering a message of love from Spirit. Eagles soar above reminding me of grace and strength. The water calms my heart and soothes my soul. Always reminded that Goddess is just a heartbeat away. No fear, only solace in this garden of light, peace, and love.

Notice that which surrounds you in beauty for it speaks to you in truth. ~Namaste

Animal Spirituality

Are there animals that seem to walk into your life often? Have you ever thought about the messages that each animal brings you? Many cultures give great meaning to these messages. Native Americans have always felt a spiritual connection to all animals. There is a deep respect and profound communication that occurs. I often see deer on my walks, black bear show up at my back door a few times a year, and as of late, the majestic eagle has been flying high and low around me. I see, listen, and stay open for Spirit to guide me through these messages.

If an animal has been showing up for you, research the meaning. You may be surprised by how in sync the message is with your life situation. Below is some of my research on the eagle.

"The eagle represents spiritual protection, carries prayers, and brings strength, courage, wisdom, illumination of spirit, healing, creation, and knowledge of magic. The eagle has the ability to see hidden spiritual truths, rising above the material to see the spiritual. The eagle has an ability to see the overall pattern, and the connection to spirit guides and teachers. The eagle represents great power and balance, dignity with grace, a connection with higher truths, intuition, and a creative spirit grace achieved through knowledge and hard work." ~Eagle Spirit Ministry

Pay attention, see, and receive.

Find Your Feather

Oftentimes, as I am moving through my walks, I come upon something of meaning to me. It may be a butterfly fluttering between the wildflowers, crickets singing in the background, or a frog leaping into the water puddles on the side of the road. But most significant to me are the feathers I find along my path. They always show up when I need them most. On a day when I'm feeling out of sorts and unsure of my direction, Spirit sends me this gift. As I'm walking along, deep in thought, I look down...and there is my feather! It always amazes me, like the first time. My heart flutters, I smile, pick it up and carry it with me as I stroke every strand, feeling the strength of Spirit. It is, a reminder that angels are always around me and God is guiding me every step of the way. I don't have to carry the heaviness or know the answers. I can let go. What a relief to truly believe that! My day always starts over with a renewed sense of gratitude and inner security.

So what is it that you find along your path that reminds you of Spirit's guiding light? Look around you, be aware and know that it is there. Feel your own perfection. You are worth being loved, you deserve to receive, and you deserve to enjoy the life that you have been given.

Every time I look at my feathers in the various special places in my home and office, my soul reconfirms my connection to Spirit and I am filled with gratitude. Look around, find your "feather," it is there for you, too!

Flutter Me Butterfly

"BUTTERFLY – denotes renewal and rejuvenation, the ability to bounce back from setbacks or disappointments, a transformation of spirituality. They stand for beauty and metamorphosis. It symbolizes the human soul."
~Meaning of the Butterfly, Dream Analysis Index

I had my yearly spirit circle meeting with my wonderful like-spirited friends recently. My dad joined our circle to give me the message of the butterfly. "You are pinning down the butterfly," he said. As I explored the meaning of the butterfly, it all made sense. Not to mention the fact that I have been talking about noticing the butterfly and searching for them on my walks. The butterfly has been utmost in my mind these past few weeks. Yes, dad knows. Dad always knows and he only confirmed my search and the deeper meaning underneath it all.

Along with the Native American culture, I too believe in the powerful messages animals and all living creatures bring to us. The next time you are presented with a life force other than human, pay attention. Observe that life, connect with the energy, and allow what Source brings to you. You may be pleasantly surprised by the outcome.

You're Right About That

"The choice to let go and let God, in a quest to eliminate our attachment to being right, is simplified with these few words: You're right about that." ~Dr. Wayne Dyer

If we could all learn to say, "You're right about that" more often, there would be so much more understanding in this world. Just saying this phrase opens you up to listen, not judge, accept, and learn. Learn that your attachment to being right isn't the answer. That is simply ego puffing out his little chest. In practicing being open you just might learn something of value.

When we have to be right, we block all other information from entering our conscious and unconscious mind. Imagine what we might miss in this stubborn process! I learn from you, you learn from me, and maybe, just maybe, we can work together and journey to a productive outcome.

Ego attachment leaves you alone and lonely. While you are sitting with yourself in your legendary mind remember that it takes love, caring, forgiveness, and giving service to others to feel whole again. We are all a part of each other, open to working and creating together. Dictation and separation only leaves pieces of fluff floating in the air. Do you choose to be whole and full, or empty and scattered? Always your choice.

So...even though I suggest you not attach to ego, if you look at me and say, "I like my ego and I have to be right!" I just might say to you, "You're right about that." Imagine the conversation that could unfold. Maybe, just maybe, we would learn from each other.

Vulnerability

"We're never so vulnerable than when we trust someone – but paradoxically, if we cannot trust neither can we find love or joy." ~Walter Anderson

To be vulnerable or not to be vulnerable? That is a question I am often asked, and my answer is never black and white. There is a time to be vulnerable, and a time to protect your emotions and your spirit. When you are in the company of someone you trust, that is the time to test your inner freedom and put yourself out there emotionally. Having these experiences allows you to grow in many ways. The more you test the limits with yourself and step out of your own box, the more you will learn and grow from those experiences. It is always nice to have a trusting friend to confide in, one who supports you unconditionally. Remember, however, we are all human and even your very best friend can let you down at times. More than likely, this union bounces back if it has a firm foundation of friendship.

A friend of mine often tells me, "I'm never trusting another guy again, they all hurt you eventually!" There are certain people and experiences that hurt you in some way, but that doesn't mean you have to give up on trusting again. Be cautious, yes. Live in fear, no. Trust your inner instincts. You know when you meet someone, or develop a relationship with them, if you need to have your guard up. Trust yourself and all of the signs that come to you. If you get a funny feeling in your gut when someone makes you a promise, pay attention. If you pull away when someone puts their arm around you, pay attention. If you look into someone's eyes and the connection is not there, pay attention. Listen to your own soul, intently.

To be vulnerable or not to be…you be the judge. Listen and pay attention to you. Always remember, however, it is not wasted time or energy if you misjudged. Pick up your pieces and learn from them. You will be much wiser the next time around. Never lose the lesson. Take the learning with you. As my friend Raven reminds me…pay attention to the signs. Always.

A Father's Love

"I loved Susan from the moment she was born, and I love her now and every minute in between. And what I dream of is a man who will discover her, and that she will discover a man who will love her, who is worthy of her, who is of this world, this time, and has the grace, compassion, and fortitude to walk beside her as she makes her way through this beautiful thing called life."
~Quote from the movie, *Meet Joe Black*

Last night, as I perused the channels, I came across what is perhaps my favorite movie of all time, *Meet Joe Black*. It has a mixture of life's checks and balances; real love, false love, anger, deception, death, and most touching to me, the love a father has for his daughter. The quote above is William Parrish's (played by Anthony Hopkins) description of the depth of a father's love. For anyone who has had a father such as this, you are blessed. You have experienced a love that has nurtured you in a way to recognize real love when it enters your life. Recognition and choice are two separate entities, however. You can be given all the love and tools available to choose wisely, but it is ultimately up to you to love yourself enough and remember what that real love felt like. Real love is unconditional, it is full of forgiveness, it is accepting and nonjudgmental, no matter what. Real love lives forever and always bounces back. Even when angry, the blow softens and is replaced with the heart. Real love is taking yourself out of the equation and wanting true happiness for the other. Real love is real.

I had a father like William Parrish. He may not have been as emotionally expressive, but his *actions* spoke louder than his words. Always there, always available, always on time. Always with his hand held out to save me from drowning, yet allowed me the freedom to learn my own lessons. Always with a full heart and never asked for anything in return. I felt the unconditional, strong love William had for Susan. My father's love, a true blessing.

Whether you had a father similar to William Parrish or not, remember to love and respect yourself enough to choose one who is capable of giving you the love you deserve. One who is worthy of you and the love you give. Your heart doesn't lie. It will tell you if real love has entered your life. Real love enhances your life and flows with effortless energy. Just as the sun provides to a blossoming flower. False love zaps all energy and leaves you depleted as you second guess all your efforts. Treat yourself like the precious flower that you are and you will attract those that treat you the same.

Our roots lay our foundation. It is up to us to choose how our garden flourishes. Plant seeds of love in your own heart and expect that love will be returned. You are worthy. You *are* love.

How Lovable Are You?

We are only as lovable as we love ourselves. Do you treat yourself with kindness and respect? Do you nurture the precious person that you are? It all begins with you. How can you expect anyone to treat you with respect if you don't believe you deserve it? We truly teach others how to treat us.

Who are you? What do you love about yourself? Look deeply within and nurture that lovely part of you that shines. That beautiful light that glows within and projects out into the world. All of us have something to offer ourselves and others. Search that pathway and follow it! You are worth every second that you pay attention to who you are, what you need, and how you can share your gifts with all you come in contact with. You are worth the time you give yourself today.

For those of you who think you are conceited for loving yourself, think again. We were all created in perfection. In loving ourselves we show our appreciation for the gift of life. To nurture your body, mind, and soul is to give thanks for this very life! It is our God-given right to feel love, happiness, and joy in our lives. Love who you are, feel kindness and compassion for all of life's experiences, let go of the illusion of control, and watch it all flow...effortlessly.

It all starts with you.

Roll Like Water

Most of us have heard the expression, "Let it roll like water off a duck's back." Imagine that duck emerging from the lake, the water beading and rolling clear off the duck with its feathery softness completely dry. Total separation from the liquid that just surrounded him. Now, imagine this same separation for you as you emerge from an environment that is drowning your energy. So many of us take on the energy, criticism, and responsibility of others. The beauty of knowing it is all an illusion is just that. You can take it on and play the scene in your head, over and over, or you can hit the eject button and release yourself. Don Miguel Ruiz speaks of this in his book, *The Four Agreements*. In the second agreement, "Don't Take Anything Personally," he reminds us that everyone has their own experiences and their own movie playing in their heads. When someone says something hurtful to you, it is almost always more about them than it is about you. They bring their life experience and expectations to the table and want to include you in their drama. It is always up to you whether you play a part in it or not. Your choice, no one else's. Remember, NO ONE has the ability to rattle you unless you give them permission!

As you separate yourself from others' opinions and control attempts, your strength builds as you connect more intensely to Source. Your beautiful bubble of Spirit protects your light and keeps the darkness at bay. You are never alone in this light. Your thoughts are safe and secure with the knowledge that you are surrounded by love and guidance. Sit in the quiet and breathe into the strength and love of Spirit. As my friend Maria often says, it reminds her of that MC Hammer song, "Can't Touch This!" Right on, Maria.

Let it roll, my friends, and the serenity never ends.

The Slower the Better

"Be not afraid of growing slowly, be afraid only of standing still." ~Chinese Proverb

Have you ever been on one of those quick-fix fad diets that promise rapid weight loss? The rapid weight loss occurs but then when the diet is over you gain the weight back and often more! This is so true of life change as well. If you are looking for a quick-fix to deal with something that has manifested itself over your lifetime, keep looking. Promises may be made, and you may find that you make some temporary changes, but over time you go back to the same old habits. This is a lesson in patience. PERMANENT CHANGE TAKES TIME. What will likely happen is that you will make a needed change, and then you will fall off track. It's okay, get back on track. The goal is not perfection; it is progress along the way. If you see that you have made some progress over time, pat yourself on the back and keep on going. In time, and it may even be years, you will look back and witness the road you have traveled. Even if you are not where you want to be yet, you are reaching your goals! In my experience, the longer it takes you to reach a goal, the better chance you have of making that lifestyle change permanently. If you don't go on a fad diet, and instead change your daily eating habits, your body will eventually get used to eating those foods and you won't desire the old foods. With slow change you are grounding and growing roots of stability. That will become your habit over time. It does take perseverance, acceptance of imperfection, and celebration!

So don't ever give up and feel as though you're a failure when you have a "hiccup" in your progress. Bring your mindset back to where it needs to be and be the tortoise on your way to victory!

Understand Nothing

A great teacher of mine once said to me, "You think too much!" At the time, I didn't really grasp the true meaning of her words, but as time went on, life's lessons taught me her message. Whenever we struggle to have all the answers and we have to figure it out, we are in trouble. That is the fight to be in control and see the world in black and white. Well guess what? There is a lot of gray in life, and as we grow older, life teaches us that lesson. Has this ever happened to you? You're moving along and all seems good. In fact, it feels so good that you begin to feel omnipotent, as though nothing can harm you. You're on cloud nine, your ego begins to grow a bit and BAM! You're thrown a curve ball and forced to fall to your knees. If you are viewing life with an open mind and heart, you will realize that this is an opportunity for learning and growth. After all, when does the growth curve happen most dramatically? When we are in pain. It is at this time that we don't have all the answers. Our ego has been knocked down a notch, and hopefully, for our own sake, humility takes a front seat. When we are humbled, we judge less and accept our surroundings more. There is a letting go that occurs when our focus reaches inward. When we accept that we aren't perfect, we will accept others and their imperfections.

So...in an effort to understand, understand nothing. Be gentle with yourself. Allow life to take its course. Know that you don't have all the answers. Be open and allow the universe to lead you. Accept change, even if it isn't your idea, follow it and find the magic life has in store for you. Enjoy every moment, and even in the painful times, know that you are exactly where you are meant to be. You are learning. You are growing. You are becoming a beautiful human being. Understand nothing.

Sensuous Healing

"Nothing can cure the senses but the soul, just as nothing can cure the soul but the senses." ~Oscar Wilde

What have you enjoyed in your life lately that has appealed to all of your senses? Sight, smell, taste, touch, and hearing are all senses of your body that require attention in order to truly appreciate life. What memories resurface when you hear a personally meaningful song, smell the scent of your favorite flower, feel the touch of a soothing massage, taste your favorite fruit, or gaze at a majestic landscape? Close your eyes and imagine...now go experience each one! Take the time out of your day to pamper yourself. No excuses. Treat yourself to what life has to offer. Go sit on the beach and pour the sunbaked sand over your legs. Spend a night at your favorite Inn and lavish in all it has to offer. Pack a sumptuous lunch and savor it as you sit under your favorite tree. Go for a car ride with all the windows open and sing at the top of your lungs, breathing in the fresh air. Cash in that spa certificate you received a year ago and completely forgot about. Book that hot air balloon ride you've always dreamed about flying in!

Whatever it is that allows you to feel ALIVE, follow it. Experience it, feel it, and love every moment of it!

It Is Written

No one writes your truth for you. It is written by your soul. Or I should say, through your soul. This is going to sound funny, but so often when I write I am half asleep. Seriously, I simply write from the heart, with my eyes half closed, thinking to myself, this isn't going to make any sense at all when I read this later. Ironically, it often makes a lot of sense, so much so I question where the words came from. In reality, I know that most of what I write is simply Spirit moving through me. I'm a conduit, open and willing to convey a message of healing. Trusting in the knowing of light.

Originally, this writing was going to be about being true to yourself and not allowing others to write your story for you. As I began, I realized that writing your truth is all about staying open and allowing. It is a partnership between you and all universal light. A meshing of pieces creating colors beyond description, but when the intermingling occurs it's so very clear. It's not about barriers, it's about abundance! Remain open and the horizons are endless.

See what happens when my eyes are half closed? It is then that I truly begin to see the light. Open yourself and trust. You will see the light, too.

Serenity Prayer

"God, grant me the serenity to accept the things I cannot change, the courage to change the things I can, and the wisdom to know the difference." ~Reinhold Niebuhr

If you break down the Serenity Prayer into sections, the message becomes clear. You cannot change others or experiences out of your control. You have the ability to change yourself, if you so wish. Oftentimes, we need to look at our own fears and drum up the courage to make the leap. Examine the difference between what is within your control and what isn't. As decisions are made, never forget your spiritual connection to the universe. This will give you the strength and inner peace as you move through each step.

Change can be difficult. Change can be easy. The Serenity Prayer has helped me through many changes in my life. The art of letting go and the courage to hold on. Listen to your own inner guidance as it connects you to the wisdom of Spirit. You will be well on your way.

The Blame Game

Take responsibility for your own actions *and* be kind to yourself. Blaming someone else for choices you make doesn't make the problem go away, it only exacerbates the issue. When you accept responsibility it eases the tension and leaves an open forum for discussion. Blaming only pushes the other party into a corner and creates a defensive stance. Thus, creating a hurricane out of a breeze. Calm the breeze with kindness toward yourself and the other person. Oftentimes, there is a cooling off period that needs to take place. If emotions are heated, I suggest you temporarily walk away from the situation and return to the topic when your emotions have stabilized.

When guilt enters the picture, our self-esteem plummets and our egos scramble to project the wrong-doing onto somebody else. I suggest there is no wrong or right, but rather choices we make to learn valuable lessons in our life. Guilt, which I have defined as "the silent killer of the soul," only stifles you on your road to growth and learning. It beats you down and throws you into the darkness where you become blinded by the shame. Allow yourself to stand up into the light and flourish despite your painful choices.

There are no mistakes in this life. Your journey is yours to live and learn from. Feel the blessings of the difficulties you tackle, hold your head high, and move on to reap the benefits of what you learned today.

Clarity

Remember that song, "I Can See Clearly Now," by Johnny Nash? For some reason, this song has been streaming through my head lately. I catch myself walking through the house singing, "I can see clearly now, the rain is gone...," and it only brings back good feelings from my past. I remember loving this song as a young girl and how it made me feel happier, somehow. It was a reminder that no matter what happened in life, the cloud would lift and the sun would shine again. Life is a continuous ebb and flow, and as we experience pain it helps to remember that the painful experience doesn't last forever. The light streaming out of the tunnel gradually becomes brighter with each step toward the healing rainbow. I've heard it said that the lesson is learned when the experience is lost. That's when clarity hits and the "aha" moment happens. That's when your thoughts are clear and your joy emanates. That's when the lesson is learned.

Do what you must to experience the lesson, dig into the trenches, build your palace and allow yourself to reap the rewards of your labor. You WILL see a bright, bright sunshiny day!

Curve Balls

Life does throw us curve balls sometimes, and it is up to us to accept or reject those curves. While on a beautiful vacation with my family on the shores of North Carolina, I was reminded of this lesson. I so much love my beach walks, taking in the surroundings and listening to the sound of the surf. The first morning of my arrival I excitedly headed out for my morning walk. Clipping along, getting my exercise in as well as taking in the scenery, I didn't think about the harm I could be doing my bare feet walking on the slanted sand. Five miles later, I felt tired but wonderful at the same time. I love feeling the sand under my feet and running through the water as it splashes my body and cools me down. What a glorious morning! Then, three hours later it hit me. My ankle didn't feel as happy as I did about that walk. In fact, it was pretty steaming mad at me! I was hobbling around by the end of the day, and the next two days. Oh I so much missed taking my beach walks. I thought about how my morning routine was all messed up, I couldn't even get my exercise in!

As I was forced to sit in the quiet, it finally dawned on me that sitting was exactly what I was meant to do and where I was meant to be. Sometimes, we push ourselves too hard and life teaches us a lesson in slowing down. There were so many wonderful insights and revelations I took in while sitting instead of walking. Don't get me wrong, both are good, but I was somehow out of balance with the sitting part. In sitting, I was able to see the seagulls instead of just watching them fly by. I was able to notice the dolphins playfully move through the water. I was able to watch my kids ride the surf and laugh with each other. I was able to read my book and escape into the characters' lives. Ideas and creativity were coming to me regarding my writing and counseling. There's so much we miss when we don't slow down and notice, watch, and listen.

I'm so very grateful for my curve ball that was thrown at me my very first day of arrival. It forced me to see and learn yet another lesson in patience and appreciation. If we could all learn to appreciate what comes our way we would be much better off. Even the curve balls you think are negative can ALWAYS be turned into a very positive learning experience. Nothing should be lost in a lesson. See it, hold it, grab on to it! Go with the flow of the universe and its messages, you will be happy you did.

What is Your Self-Worth?

It's interesting how we put a value on our homes, cars, businesses, financial investments and various material things, but do we value ourselves? When was the last time you checked in with your own inner bank? When you think about it now, how full is it? In order to fill your inner bank you need to attend to many aspects of your life. Here is a mini list of inner fulfillment reminders:

~NO is a beautiful word. Say it when you know it is the right thing for you.

~Take some quiet time to yourself every day.

~In relationships, have boundaries with those that are prone to take more than they give and psychically drain you.

~Stop attempting to have emotionally connected relationships with love interests that are not able to connect emotionally. You CANNOT and WILL NOT change others, they have to want to change themselves.

~Hug and kiss your kids and your loved ones every time you think about it.

~Call a friend that you trust and vent, and allow them to vent with you. Relationships do require give and take, after all. If no venting is needed, just call, just because.

~Pay attention to your intuition. Your "gut" most often guides you in the direction you are meant to follow. Don't ignore it.

~Find employment/career that suits you and one that allows you to feel productive and satisfied at the end of the day.

~Exercise to the level you feel comfortable and choose a form that brings a smile to your face!

~Eat lots of fruits and veggies, and drink plenty of water every day.

~Be kind and gentle with yourself and remember that you are worth every positive, nurturing action you take to fill your inner tank!

~And lastly, but certainly not least, incorporate a spiritual practice into your everyday life. Pray, meditate, experience nature and your connectedness to it...LISTEN and pay attention to messages that come to you from God, angels, spirit guides, nature, and all that speaks to you. Be open, be aware, be love.

The Feminine Rests While the Masculine Swims

When my radio show came to a close, I walked out one door and through another, feeling the reminder of balance that is required to create wholeness in my life. An abundance of nurturing, giving energy went into the creation of *Help, Hope & Healing*, another baby in my life, and then it came time to move on.

On my last show, Dream Momma unraveled one of my dreams; a journey dream, as she called it. As always, she was right on as I began walking new roads leading to the excitement of the unknown. While my latest endeavor unfolds, Dream Momma calls out my masculine side to strengthen his muscles, pull up his boot straps, and get to work! In my dream, I am swimming to the "boat" carrying the next level of my life. My right side is strong, stroking vigorously, while my left side rests, gathering her own strength which she has given so freely.

And now, as I gaze out my window at the red mountainous terrain of Sedona, I feel the strength building within. Ready for my next adventure. Ready to feel the earth below me again, rumbling through my veins, heart pulsating, guiding me to the next journey of my soul. Allowing, open, letting go…

The Gift of Crisis

What difficulty have you experienced in life that has brought you to your next level? Every passage, every step you take contributes to the person you are today. It is often the most painful times that create a strength within and pushes us to tackle that which we fear the most. We tell ourselves, "Hey, if I can make it through that the next task can't be so hard." And often it isn't. Every crisis in our life can be turned into a gift. It's all in how you view your potential as you move through the difficulty. Always remind yourself that "this too shall pass," and you will be better off for it. I realize it's not easy to think positively when something negative is happening around you, but think in those terms and it will pass quicker than you can imagine. It's simply a matter of perspective, and we receive exactly what we perceive.

Acknowledge all gifts the universe sends to you...joyful, painful, blissful, and monumental. Express gratitude for the opportunity to build upon your spiritual core and reach your potential. The sky is the limit!

Bless Every Experience

Every step we take is an experience in this life. There are no mistakes, no coincidences, and no failures. With each road traveled we learn and expand through the beautiful, the painful, and all in between. No labels are needed as good or bad, it simply is what it is. What did you learn through your last experience? Was something or someone presented to you to test your strength or your capacity for love? Perhaps your heart opened inward and you learned to love yourself. All situations and relationships create the precious person you are. Allow yourself to feel the emotions streaming through you and your energy will not be lost. If you must move into darkness to find light, so be it. Experience it, live it, ride it! You will flourish with every courageous step you take.

If amends need to be made, make them. Don't be afraid to push your ego aside and simply say you're sorry. An apology travels a long way when it is sincere. All negative energy disappears when the air is cleared and you are able to move on. Untie your past, live in the present, and look forward to your future. You are meant to ride your wave freely.

Bless it all. Change is constant, and with change is the opportunity for growth. Grab a hold of your vine and fly!

Secret Words

My wise old friend once told me a secret. She told me if I regularly used 12 words in my vocabulary my light would shine brighter. Actually, scientifically, she explained that using these words would affect how my brain processes my view of life. As we are taught the perception and meaning of these words in our culture, you can understand why verbalizing them often would embed positive visions in our minds. For those of you who know me, you know I use these words often. Every time I write, voice, or think of them, I can't help but light up! Their definition warms my heart, and so does the memory of that wise old woman who illuminated my life.

Salubrious	**Wondrous**
Beauteous	**Luminous**
Miraculous	**Numinous**
Mysterious	**Humorous**
Glorious	**Anonymous**
Joyous	**~The Silence**
Harmonious	

XIII.
Earth Angels and Beyond

Recognize and give thanks to all angels that come to you today. Some walk this earth, some are more ethereal in nature, others make themselves known in your everyday existence. Notice that nudge that comes to you in your sleep, or that feather that lightly touches your cheek. It is very likely your angel giving you a message of love, hope, guidance, faith, and letting you know you're not alone. Never alone. Always wrapped in angels' wings…

The Great Ship of Friendship

**"Piglet sidled up to Pooh from behind. "Pooh!" he whispered. "Yes, Piglet?" "Nothing," said Piglet, taking Pooh's paw. "I just wanted to be sure of you."
~A.A. Milne**

Isn't it a beautiful feeling when you know you can count on someone? If you can add on one hand those you know will be there for you, no matter what, you are blessed. Friendship isn't a one way street of taking, it is a back and forth motion of giving and receiving. A feeling of warmth that is indescribable in words. My angels not only surround me in the Spirit world, they gather around me here on the earth plane. How blessed are we when we find this connection, true love in all its purity.

Thank you, my friends, for providing comfort when the rest of the world dims to dark. You keep me on my light path, soul connections banded together, paving the way. Wrapped in angels' wings.

Bouncing my love back to you...

Wings Take Flight

Wings may break

Feelings get hurt

Sadness invades our space

But the Soul is always intact

Guiding you

Carrying you

Loving you

Sit up, breathe

Stand up, walk

Hold your head high

Strap on your wings

And FLY!

If you have just experienced a difficult time in your life, know that there was meaning in every painful feeling you encountered. Hold the pain in your hands, welcome it, caress it, and then release it like fairy dust into the universe. Your angels will grab hold and carry the weight for you. Let it go. Trust and believe that you will carry on, learning through your lesson, continually growing...finding your new soul home to settle into.

Your wings are waiting...gather your breath, rev your engines, and soar to your next destination!

Thank You

Don't forget to say "thank you" today. Whether it be the clerk at the grocery store, your co-worker who rubs you the wrong way, your dearest friend, your mom, your teenager who has had attitude with you for the 10th time today, your pastor, your employee, your ex-spouse...the list goes on. Look them in the eye, smile, and simply say, "Thank you." You will be amazed by how it lightens any tension that may be between you, and how it enhances the bond that already exists. When we are kind toward others, and appreciative of them, there is an inner warmth that begins to expand throughout your body and soul.

Has someone extended a kindness toward you lately? Reciprocate with a thank you note, email, or call. Is it someone's birthday today? Take the time to go to the store, pick out a birthday card, and send it. Have you been thinking about a loved one? Pick up the phone and call them. We all get busy in this fast-paced life, but it's the time when we STOP and thank those around us that it becomes special and light-filled.

When we live life with gratitude we receive fields of beautiful flowers. Open your arms and enjoy the love that surrounds you!

The Hands of Friendship

"Love is blind, friendship is clairvoyant." ~anonymous

Friendship is the true foundation of any relationship. When we hold hands, instead of hearts, we allow those we love the freedom to expand and spread their wings. A true friend is someone who walks in when all others leave; no attachment, no judgment, just pure love and acceptance. She is one who will sit with you for hours while you laugh, cry, and work through life's challenges. He is one you may not talk to for years, then you pick up the phone and it's as if your conversation never skipped a beat. You know who your true friends are. You feel it from the bottom of your heart to the top of your soul. True friends remain through a lifetime, no matter where you are, no matter how far.

A real friend is not blinded by the fog of being "in love." She won't tell you what you want to hear, she will tell you what you need to hear. She will lead with honesty and call you on your flaws. Not to hurt you, only to help you. Just as you will do the same for her. In this give and take relationship you learn from each other; one step at a time, one lesson at a time, holding hands along this path called life.

Friendships and Funny Bones

I asked my girls last night, "What should I write about, girlfriend fun, manifestation, or ego and attachment?" Girlfriend fun won, hands down. Out of the mouths of babes. The other topics will come again, but I think we all need a reminder to surround ourselves with those we love and simply insert FUN into our lives!

I recently took a weekend girlfriend trip to New York City. How long had it been since I sang in the car at the top of my lungs? I must say, Suzy and I harmonized pretty well. Remembering all the words to Billy Joel, Dan Fogelberg, The Eagles, just to name a few. Red lights in the city, cell phone snapshot time! No, not of the sights, of our own silly poses. And it didn't stop when we joined Marjie; more pouty face, late night silly shots to come. We were giddy and exhausted, and yes, completely enjoying each other. There's something to say about friendships that bring out the "girl" in you. It allows you to be completely free with your authentic self. No judgment, no have-to's or supposed-to's, only total acceptance. Add doses of laughter and your package is complete.

When I take my "Round Robin" trip with my girlfriends from high school every year, we enjoy life to the fullest! So many ups and downs, so many wonderful memories, some wild, fun times, some sad times…and always there for each other. We've traveled to Boston, Maine, the Finger Lakes, Lake Placid, the hills of New York, Sedona, Las Vegas, Santa Cruz, Napa, and my home. Many hikes, hot tubs, wild rides, late night talks, and interesting meets along the way tell the tale of the depth of our friendship. This spring, Heather, Louise and I will be circling back around to Boston and continue our road trip into New Hampshire and Cape Cod. I see a few days of spontaneity on the horizon!

Don't pass it by. Call a friend today, have a laugh, remember what brought you together, and relive it. I'm so very thankful for ALL my girlfriends and the joy they bring to my life. I am blessed! You know who you are, sending you love and hugs today and every day...now let's get out and PLAY!!!

Joie de Vivre!

What is it that brings you true joy? Try sitting with this question; close your eyes, breathe into it, and think and feel what brings you happiness. If nothing comes to you at first, that's okay. Just allow what does come and be patient with yourself. If you practice this exercise daily it will eventually reveal itself. Pay attention when you laugh, smile, and feel the warmth inside of you during a thought. It just might be something you would like to incorporate into your life.

One of the things that brings me joy is dance. It's a fun movement of the body with music that allows me to feel and connect with friends. And believe me, there are plenty of laughs in a room full of women ages 18 to 60 with different levels of dance experience. During one class, my friend yells out in the middle of a dance that she's hungry for a hamburger! Needless to say, there were a lot of laughs in that room that night. It did get me craving a strawberry milkshake, however, and I promptly got one on my way home. Anyway, the point is, how you feel after exercising your mind, body, spirit, and emotion is beyond any high an outer substance can bring you. And the only side effect? Joie!

Reiki Ricardo

So I walk into dance class, ask where my friend is, and the whole class blurts out, "She's with Reiki Ricardo!" I laugh knowing there's a joking lining with these girls, but yes, I take the bait and ask, "And WHO is Reiki Ricardo?" Our wonderful comic tells me that my friend is at her Reiki class but they kid with her telling her she spends too much time with Reiki! For those of you who remember *I Love Lucy*, many images pop up, don't they? Ricky with the big band doing his mambo jumbo, and all of the hysterics of Lucy. We carry on with some big laughs between our dance steps, filling the room with joy.

Coming back down to earth, Reiki is truly a wonderful practice and soothing inner belief system. My friend, Amanda, is a Reiki Master. After one treatment with her and I feel like I just had an intense full body massage. So relaxed and centered am I. I will leave it to the Masters to describe exactly what a Reiki treatment is, but my version is that it is a vibrational energy from the practitioner that treats the body and energy force of the client. The Master's hands are raised a few inches off the body as it scans all chakras.

I have always loved *The Reiki Principles*. Amanda has them framed in her office adjacent to mine. As I finish my workday, I often take a quick look at them as a reminder of a kind, compassionate, healthy way of living. Just for today keeps us in the present. One step at a time, one moment at a time.

The Reiki Principles

~Just for today I will give thanks for my many blessings.

~Just for today I will not worry.

~Just for today I will not be angry.

~Just for today I will do my work honestly.

~Just for today I will be kind to my neighbor and every living thing.

Confessions of a Spa Junkie

Okay, I confess, put me in a spa full of personal pamperings and I'm like a kid in a candy store. I'll have one of those, two of those, and five of those! Everything about a spa rejuvenates and relaxes me, and centers my soul. From the music to the aromatherapy to the sound of the waterfall, not to mention the amazing treatments. Massages, facials, pedicures, manicures, and special treats like mud baths, "lavender dreams," and "the balancing waters ritual."

That being said, it is important to keep even healthy activities in perspective to avoid an unhealthy environment. Anything taken to an extreme can cause chaos and conflict. If I went to the spa every day, all day, my bank account would be empty and my family would be neglected.

Find that something that feeds your soul. As long as it is healthful and fulfilling, and your life is in balance, you will feel the benefits in all aspects of your daily living. After a massage, I am so much more receptive and kinder to those around me. My physical, mental, emotional, and spiritual components are in sync and my intuition is clear. All pathways are open to the offerings of the universe.

What is it that brings a smile to your heart and a jump in your step? Take a dip into the sweet delicacies of life and feel the freedom!

A Breath of Fresh Air

Here's a little exercise for you today. Throughout the day, focus on your breathing. Whether you have a busy day or a calm day, I ask that you consciously stop, sit or stand up straight, close your eyes or just focus on one point, and breathe in through your nose and out your mouth. Allow your belly to expand as you breathe in order to allow the oxygen to flow through your whole body. Do this for as long as you feel comfortable, several times throughout the day.

At the end of the day, sit quietly, look around at your surroundings, and be conscious of how you feel. Any difference? My guess is YES!

Calm your mental, emotional, physical, and spiritual self today. It's worth your time.

The Grateful Heart

Give thanks to Spirit every day and allow that glorious energy to work inside of you. When we clutter our mind with chatter it blocks all pathways to our inner peace and intuitive abilities. Allow the peaceful, positive energy to guide you and you will be amazed by what shows up. Sit in the quiet, meditate, pray...send out gratitude for every experience and learning lesson in life. The more we send out loving energy the more we are surrounded by love.

The warmth of gratitude allows your soul to shine, inside and out. Enjoy the glow!

XIV.
 *Bringing it Home*

In knowing who you are there is no need to believe what others tell you to be. There is no need to hide from yourself and the world. There is no need to live the lie as you spin out of control. There is only a need to honor your authentic self. Who is that, you ask? Look in the mirror, reach further than your face, and Spirit will show you the way. ~

Simple Rejuvenation

Rejuvenation isn't something that just happens, it is a process of creating boundaries and letting go of old energy that has served its purpose. Recently, I've released some things and people in my life that were once fulfilling and energetic, but there comes a time when all must come to an end for the new to enter through the closed door. It is the opening to the new that allows us to continue our journey and expand to deeper depths than before.

Spread your wings and fly among the truth seekers. In between the quiet pieces of time you will find beauty in the early morning sunrise, the smile upon a child's face, the grace of a swan on a silvery lake, taking you to the stillness of your original soul. To BE. Simply rejuvenating.

Vertical Coffin

I once had a wise old crone ask me, "What are you doing to make your life count? Are you listening to your heart, your soul's purpose, or are you just going through the motions of your daily routine?" She then went on to say, in her firm motherly voice, that I am not to wither away in this life. "Wake up! Enjoy it, follow your heart, listen to your intuition, and don't you dare let ANYONE pull you away from that!" Words of wisdom from a woman who lived life, and still lives inside of me.

Have you ever seen the movie, *Night of the Living Dead*? I remember seeing it in high school with a group of friends and I still remember it vividly to this day. A cluster of people awake from the dead are wandering aimlessly through the town. They are alive, but dead. And although it was kind of a creepy movie, it had a message. So many of us appear to have no direction and feel extremely lost inside. If you get nothing else from this writing, get this, you are NEVER lost! There is so much of value inside each and every one of us. You need only to look, and see, and act. Make that choice to have joy in your life! Instead of running that errand today (like you do every day), go for a hike, ride your horse, get a massage, go to a movie, go to a bookstore and sit in a big chair and read, go skiing, go to lunch with a friend, sign up for that conference, roll in the snow with your kids...whatever your heart's desire. That errand can wait until tomorrow, and so can your vacuum cleaner. Your "to do" list never ends, don't wait so you can finish it, break it up.

Throw down your broom and get out there and have fun! You've got nothing to lose, and so much to gain.

Manifesting Your Heart's Desire

"The power of intention is the power to manifest, to create, to live a life of unlimited abundance, and to attract into your life the right people at the right moments." ~Dr. Wayne Dyer

Whatever it is you wish to bring into your life, you have the ability and power to manifest that desire. What is it you are requesting to enhance your experience of daily living? Set that intention and say to yourself, "I am creating this business," "I am attracting positive people into my life," "I send out love and receive love," whatever it is you desire can, and will, be manifested with each step you take. Write down your intention, tack it on a poster board, look at it every day, imagine yourself already there, and remind yourself that you are able to bring to you whatever it is you desire! Don't sit around waiting for someone to do it for you, reach deep within and move to the challenge. Put in your energy and hard work. When your intention comes to fruition you will feel the joy of accomplishment. The awareness that you manifested this through your dedication and connection to all universal energy only makes it sweeter.

You have the power to create, and draw to you, all that awaits you in the universe. Never forget that. You have strength. You have ability. You have the power of intention. Focus on your dreams, do the work, send it out to the universe, and watch it come alive!

The Giving Tree

Imagine yourself as a tree that forever grows and forever gives. The giving is unconditional, there is no attachment to outcomes, you give simply to give. You give because it fulfills you and gives you more purpose in your own life. When the leaves fall it is time to replenish your soul and give to yourself. It is a time of healing, going inward, and growing. We take this time because we know if we only give to others we will eventually feel tired and depleted. There is a time when we need to replenish our own soul in order to have a full tank of love to give.

How do you fill your tank? Who, what, where, and how do you fill yourself? It may simply be reading a book in quiet time, or extravagantly flying to a deserted island for a week! It may be going to a movie, spa, or bookstore. It may be going for a walk in the woods or going to the craft store to find a project to work on. It may be sitting outside and feeling the sun shine on your face. It may be taking a bath and locking the door, telling your kids this is your time. Be creative and tune in to what brings contentment and peace to your life.

When you do give, please remember to give freely. No attachment, no conditions. Many of us think of giving in terms of what we will get back. If you have this mindset you will often be disappointed and you will never feel filled. Never. You will feel as though your tank is always empty because you set yourself up to depend on others for fulfillment. Start with yourself first. You are the only one who can fill you! If you truly understand the act of giving and kindness, you will never feel empty. You give because it makes you feel good. No expectations. Simply the act of giving.

Give, drop your leaves, replenish yourself, and then give again. The giving tree.

The Gift of Humility

When I think back on experiences I've had in my life, I think of two things I've learned; humility, and, the more I learn the less I know. In my 20s, I looked at life through a black and white lens, believing there had to be an answer for everything. Today, after experiencing numerous challenges, I've found a kaleidoscope of colors intermingling in every combination. There is no "one answer," there is only what is. When we learn to let go and trust this process, life begins to flow effortlessly.

If you are someone who has jumped some free-falls in life and have felt that deep sensation of pain, you will relate to what I'm about to say. It brought you humility. It brought you to an understanding that you aren't perfect, and yet, you are beautifully perfect in your imperfection. Difficult life experiences aren't meant to condemn you and remind you of what a terrible person you are, they are meant to stop you in your tracks long enough to reach deep down and touch that part of your soul you have neglected. They are meant to bring you to your knees, realize you don't have all the answers, and ask Spirit to guide you. Have you been there? Where you feel like you just can't handle it anymore? That's when we are humbled, and when we truly learn. If we accept this newfound wisdom, that's when we finally LIVE love and compassion for ourselves and others. Not just talk the talk but really walk the walk.

I'm a much better therapist today than I was in my younger years because I have lived. I no longer struggle to have all the answers for my clients, I'm simply a guide. It's amazing to watch the process flower as I love them through it; allowing them to expand, allowing acceptance of themselves and others, allowing their unlearning and learning. It's yet another humbling experience.

I'm filled with gratitude today, having had all of the challenges and deep pain in my life. I'm a better person for it. Softer, more understanding, less judgmental, and certainly happier. Life is good, we simply need to look at it through the eyes of our soul.

The Ocean's Edge

"You've been walking the ocean's edge,
Holding up your robes to keep them dry.
You must dive naked under,
And deeper under,
A thousand times deeper!"
~Rumi

There is something to say about the power of the unconscious mind. As we open this tunnel and dive deeper into the heart of our souls, our true experiences become unearthed, revealing themselves enough to catch and release. Providing you the opportunity to gather what still serves you and allowing what doesn't to fall to the bottom of the deep, dark ocean.

If you feel as though you are lost, and there is no escape from the closed tunnel of your mind, think again. You are more powerful than your conscious thoughts will lead you to believe. You have the power to change. You have the ability to recreate. You are here to live the light of your soul.

Dive deep. Unearth your truths, bury your lies, and you will see your light.

Fini

As I feel the warmth of the sun on my shoulders, looking out at the sparkling water dancing on the Atlantic Ocean, I think about all the days that have brought me here. The highlights, mixed with delight and difficulties, all meant to bring me to the present. No regrets in understanding that life is made up of light that dims to dark at times. The important piece to remember is this; what did you learn from it and what did you find necessary to unlearn?

Life is a balance, a juggling act that forces you to keep an eye on every choice thrown into the air. When one choice becomes your main focus, the rest of your life falls to the ground. Pay attention to all pieces of your life and take time to nurture every petal of the beautiful flower you were born to be. This includes giving, receiving, boundaries, caregiving, healthy living, and all we discussed in this book. To live in YOUR truth is to live in health.

Honor your authentic self and all will fall magically into place, one feather at a time.

Go Forward with Courage

"When you are in doubt, be still, and wait;

When doubt no longer exists for you, then go forward with courage.

So long as mists envelop you, be still;

Be still until the sunlight pours through and dispels the mists.

–As it surely will. Then act with courage."

~Ponca Chief White Eagle

Photo Credits

"Self-Love" ~ Becca Brennen in the beautiful hills of the Finger Lakes Region in New York. Photograph by Kelley Brennen.

"Soul Connectors" ~ Cassie Burdick, Paige DeRichie, Kelley Brennen, Becca Brennen, and Rachel Brennen braiding hair. Photograph by Michael Brennen.

"Letting Love In" ~ Creation and photograph by Kelley Brennen.

"Allowing the Unknown" ~ Kelley Brennen letting go in the deep of the Atlantic Ocean. Photograph by Kelley Brennen.

"Body and Mind" ~ Lexi Kirk, Cassie Smith, and Becca Brennen feeling the excitement of the Color Run race in Rochester, New York. Photograph by Paige DeRichie.

"In My Life" ~ Becca Brennen, Cynthia Brennen, Kelley Brennen, and Rachel Brennen in Palm Beach Shores, Florida. Photograph by Susan Daubner.

"Spirit Song" ~ My view at the beginning of my walk. Miraculous nature. A big thank you to my brother, Tim Weintraub, for lending me his artistry and enhancing the beauty in this photograph I took one glorious morning.

"Earth Angels and Beyond" ~ Angel Rachel Brennen in tunnel through Cayuga Lake State Park, Seneca Falls, New York. Photograph by Becca Brennen.

"Bringing it Home" ~ Cayuga Lake sunrise. Photograph by Cynthia Brennen.

All other chapter photographs by Cynthia Brennen.

About the Author

Photograph by Jeff Fasano

Cynthia Brennen has her master's degree in social work, and is licensed in the state of New York, where she enjoys her private practice in counseling. Much of Cynthia's therapy focuses on the balance of mind, body, spiritual, and emotional wellness. Cynthia enjoys writing about overall health, lessons of the heart, and her own spiritual journey. She hosted and created her talk radio show, *Help, Hope & Healing* (2010-2012), where she assisted many along their journey toward healing. She lives in the beautiful Finger Lakes Region of New York with her husband and three daughters. Website: **www.CynthiaBrennen.com**